THE CHRISTIAN VISION

GOD AND MAN: PERSPECTIVES ON CHRISTIANITY IN THE 20TH CENTURY

THE CHRISTIAN VISION

GOD AND MAN: PERSPECTIVES ON CHRISTIANITY IN THE 20TH CENTURY

Michael Bauman, Executive Editor
Lissa Roche and Lorna Busch, General Editors

Hillsdale College Press
Books by the Hillsdale College Press include the Christian
Vision series; the Champions of Freedom series; and other works.

The views expressed in this volume are not necessarily the views of
Hillsdale College.

The Christian Vision series
GOD AND MAN
© 1995 by the Hillsdale College Press
Hillsdale, Michigan 49242

Printed in the United States of America

Photo: St. Patrick's Cathedral, New York City, Copyright 1994,
Ulrike Welsch

First printing 1995

Library of Congress Catalog Card Number 95-078334
ISBN 0-916308-68-5

Contents

Introduction

The end of the 20th century marks the passage of two thousand years of Christianity. Thus, as we embark on a new century and a new millennium, we reflect not only on recent human history, but on the history of the divine-human encounter.

Militant secularists make many charges against religion, among them: that it is "the opiate of the masses" and that millions of victims have suffered and died on its altar. Yet, to believers, religion is liberation rather than oppression; it saves lives and yields the most inspiring examples of peace and good-will the world has ever seen.

Christians teach that if we truly wish to know ourselves, we must first know Christ, for He is the touchstone, the inter-pretive key, to the world around us and the souls within us. Just how well have we sought to know Him in the 20th century? The answer is far from clear. Never has disbelief, whether ex-pressed as atheism, agnosticism, secularism, or some other "ism," been stronger. One of the greatest of modern Christian writers, C.S. Lewis, was pessimistic when he wrote that the 20th century was the dawn of a "post-Christian age." Yet the evangeli-cal resurgence of recent decades seems to suggest that God is "making a comeback" and that Christianity is indeed flourish-ing. Christianity has even been credited as the cause of the fall of communism in Eastern Europe and the Soviet Union.

What is the relationship between God and man and be-tween Christianity and history in the 20th century? The essays in this volume attempt to answer such questions.

1

They are based on presentations delivered during Hillsdale College's Center for Constructive Alternatives seminar, "God and Man: Perspectives on Christianity in the 20th Century," held in November 1994.

September 1995   The Editors
Hillsdale College

The Chronicle of an Undeception

Michael Bauman

Michael Bauman is a professor of theology and culture and director of Christian Studies at Hillsdale College. He is also a lecturer and tutor in Renaissance literature and theology as well as associate dean at the Centre for Medieval and Renaissance Studies in Oxford. He has been book review editor for *The Journal of the Evangelical Theological Society* for eight years. He is the current president of the Evangelical Philosophical Society.

Formerly an editorial assistant at *Newsweek,* a pastor, chairman of the general education program at Northeastern Bible College, and an associate professor of religion at Fordham University, Dr. Bauman is the author of more than thirty articles and ten books, including *Pilgrim Theology: Taking the Path of Theological Discovery, Roundtable: Conversations with European Theologians, A Scripture Index to John Milton's* De Doctrina Christiana, *Milton's Arianism,* and editor or co-editor of *Are You Politically Correct? Debating America's Cultural Standards, The Best of the Manion Forum,* and Hillsdale's *Christian Vision* series.

> "The central myth of the sixties was that [its] wretched excess was really a serious quest for new values."
>
> —George Will

I. The Tragic Vision of Life

I confess to believing at one time or another nearly all the pervasive and persistent fantasies of the sixties. In the words of Joni Mitchell's anthem for the Woodstock nation, I thought all I had to do was "get back to the land to set my soul free." I thought that flowers had power, that love could be free, and that the system was to blame. By 1968, I had the whole world figured out. I knew the cause of every evil—America—and I knew the solution to every problem—freedom and tolerance.

If truth be told, of course, I knew nothing, at least nothing

3

worth knowing. I knew how to posture, but not how to stand. I knew how to protest, but not how to protect. I knew how to work up an impressive case of moral outrage, but I didn't know morality. I knew about peace, but I didn't know enough to fight for it. I knew about self-indulgence, self-preservation, self-esteem, and self-expression, but I didn't know about self-sacrifice and self-control.

Worse still, I didn't even know myself. I didn't know what Socrates knew about me—that I entered this world in a state of total and seamless ignorance, and that my ignorance could never be breached as long I remained blissfully unaware of it. I didn't know what St. Augustine knew about me—that the well of my soul was poisoned, and that whatever was down in the well would come up in the bucket. St. Augustine also knew this about my soul: No matter how hard it tried, no matter where it looked, it could never find its rest anywhere but in God. I didn't know what Edmund Burke knew about me—that no government could fix what ailed me, either by the things it did or by the things it did not. The most any state could do was to help protect me from myself and from others. Most importantly, however, I didn't know that I was Everyman. When I learned that, I stopped being a liberal. My deepest problems, like those of all persons, are not susceptible to government solution—a rock-hard fact that explodes the pretensions of the left and its allegedly omnicompetent state.

Like almost all dissidents of my generation, I was a protester without a plan and a visionary without a vision. I had not yet learned that you see only what you are able to see, and I was able to see only the egalitarian, relativistic, self-gratifying, superstitions of the secular, wayward left. Please do not think that this was simply a case of prelapsarian innocence. It was not. It was ignorance and it was evil, although I would have denied it at the time.

Only slowly did I come to understand that my fellow dissidents and I had taken for ourselves the easiest and least productive of all tasks, that of denigrator. And only slowly did I come to understand that to destroy is easy, that to build is hard, and that to preserve is hardest of all.

But it was worse even than that, because my fellow dissidents and I were blind to the most obvious truths, especially to what Russell Kirk and others have called the tragic vision of life—the profound realization that evil is not something "out there," it is something "in here." The tragic vision of life arises from the fact that we are flawed—deeply, desperately, tragically flawed—and we cannot be trusted. We are broken at the soul; our defect is life wide and heart deep. Though we are capable of reason, because of our selfish passions and our moral weaknesses, we are rarely reasonable. We ourselves are what is chiefly wrong with the world. We are this planet's most malignant and enduring ailment. We have our dignity, to be sure, but we have our horror as well. I can tell you this: I did not wake up until I met the enemy face to face. I met him in the mirror. We all do.

I had to learn to stare squarely into that face in the mirror, into the face of hard, fallen reality, and not to flinch. I did not, in fact I could not, comprehend the tragic vision of life until I learned that the problem of the human heart is at the heart of the human problem. Once I examined with care and honesty the habits of my own heart and those of my dissident friends, I learned that C.S. Lewis was right: to be one of the sons of Adam or the daughters of Eve is both glory enough to raise the head of the lowest beggar and shame enough to lower the head of the highest king. I am a human being. That is my wealth; that is my poverty.

Before that undeception, I was like all other cultural and political liberals. I had fallen prey to what Jeane Kirkpatrick identified as the error of "misplaced malleability." I thought that human institutions could be reshaped at will to fit the plans already existing inside my head. It cannot be done. Human institutions arise from human action; human action arises from human nature; and human nature is notoriously intractable. Apart from the grace of God, human nature cannot be fixed, no matter how badly it needs fixing. I finally learned that my deepest need was not more freedom, on the one hand, and not more government, on the other. I needed the grace and guidance of God. Until I understood that, I remained shamelessly superficial.

I had to put my insipid and airy romanticism where it

belonged, on the burgeoning junk pile of the fatally flawed and conclusively overthrown fantasies to which the human mind seems continually to give rise. Not romanticism but religion, not Byron but the Bible, not poetry but Paul, not Voltaire but virtue, not trends but tradition, not idealism but ideas, not genius but grace, not freedom but faith could cure me. I had to exchange Wordsworth for the Word and revolution for repentance. Thus, while some of the things I valued were useful and good, they were not properly fundamental. I had to put first things first.

The tragic vision of life humbled me. From it I learned that it was not my prerogative to invent wisdom and virtue. That had already been done. My responsibility was to listen to the One who invented them and to those whom He taught. Wisdom and virtue, I had to learn, were not born with my generation, or with Rousseau's, or Matthew Arnold's, or even Eugene McCarthy's. I had to learn in the last half of the twentieth century what was already old news even in the days of Jeremiah, the ancient prophet, who wrote, "Stand at the crossroads, and look, and ask for the ancient paths, where the good way lies; and walk in it, and find rest for your souls" (Jer. 6:16).

Wisdom is found by walking the "ancient paths." Those "ancient paths" led through the wilderness, through the sea, even through the valley of the shadow of death, and not through Berkeley, not Columbia, not the Village, not Watts, not Haight-Ashbury, not Altamont, and not Woodstock.

The tragic vision of life also taught me that order is the most fundamental of all political and social needs. Because it is, I learned that the police are not pigs. They never were, and are not now, an occupying army intent upon destroying my freedom. Quite the opposite; imperfect as they sometimes are, the police are the guardians of freedom and the paid protectors of life and property. In the line of duty, some of them even die for me. The tragic vision of life taught me that you cannot reject authority—whether civil, familial, cultural or divine— and yet live in an orderly world. When you "off the pigs," (of whatever sort), you give birth to an outlaw culture, not to freedom. To live outside the rules, to live outside authority, to live without the wisdom of the ages and of God, is to court slavery and death. Enforceable law and law enforcement are requirements of the first rank. Because human nature is what it is, without great volumes of enforceable law, freedom is impossible. As Dean Clarence Manion observed in the very last line he wrote before his death in 1979, "a society that is not held together by its teaching and observance of the laws of Almighty God is unfit for human habitation and doomed to destroy itself."

When is freedom not enough? Every time truth and righteousness are at stake. In a fallen world, that is almost always. Freedom must be exercised according to the dictates of truth and virtue, never the other way round. Freedom must be limited by the demands of justice, love and revelation. The most important consideration regarding any action is not "Is it free?" but "Is it good?" When I learned that, I stopped being a libertarian. Freedom, furthermore, is an incomplete concept. Whenever someone insists upon freedom, you must ask "Freedom to do what?" You must ask that question because freedom, like tyranny, has its unintended and unforeseen consequences, some of which are colossally vile. In passing, I name but one—abortion.

From the tragic vision of life I learned that you have to do what is right whether it suits you or not. In the sixties, we hardly did anything that did not suit us. I also learned that the enemy is not the CIA, not the FBI, and not the GOP; it's the NEA, NOW, NBC, ABC, CBS, CNN, DNC, WCC and NPR, indeed, the entire grab bag of alphabetized, leftist subverters of culture, of tradition, and of revelation. I learned that those who deprive themselves of the wisdom of Western tradition are no more free than a baby abandoned by its parents to do as it pleases. I learned that politics is not about equality, but justice; that personal action is not about freedom, but righteousness; and that sex is not about pleasure, but love and privilege and posterity.

These things and more I learned from the tragic vision of life. I commend them to you. They taught me that in many ways the sixties were twisted and misshapen.

The sixties are over, and it's a good thing. The sixties were a bad idea, if for no other reason than because the sixties had no ideas, only selfish desires hiding behind the shallow slogans and freelance nihilism emblazoned on psychedelic bumper stickers, slogans like "I dissent, therefore I am." The only things about which we were intellectually modest in the sixties were the claims of objective truth. We seemed unable to wrap our minds around even the most obvious ideas. We seemed unable to realize, for example, that you cannot raise your consciousness until you have one. The sixties were perhaps the most unconscious decade in centuries. It was a time of suffocating intellectual mediocrity, from which our nation has not yet recovered.

II. Sixties *Redivivus*

I can imagine a young person reading these remarks and wondering, "This all might be well and good, but what does it have to do with me? I wasn't even alive in the sixties."

My answer is simply this: While the sixties are over, they are not dead, not by a long shot. They live, indeed they thrive, not only in the White House juvenocracy, but in the faculty lounges and endowed chairs of nearly every college and university in the United States. Tenured faculty members everywhere have traded their tie-dyed T-shirts and their bell bottom jeans for a cap and gown. Those faculty members are the entrenched purveyors of an unexamined and indefensible hand-me-down Marxism, and of what Allan Bloom called "nihilism with a happy ending." They have become paid agents of the very colleges and universities they once tried to burn to the ground, and not because they gave up on the dreams of the sixties. What they failed to do as protesters they have succeeded in doing as professors. Quite possibly they have done it to you, because the entire teaching profession, from the pre-kindergarten level to the post-graduate, has become a political captive of the cultural left. Like roving street gangs prowling the halls of academe, power hungry bands of leftist professors everywhere have instigated countless institutional turf wars, most of which they have won. They have succeeded in burying the accumulated wisdom of the ages in the name of learning; in overthrowing academic freedom in the name of tolerance; in stifling debate in the name of openness; in exalting egalitarianism above all other ideas in the name of equality; and in segregating and tribalizing the university, the nation, and the culture by gender, by age, by religion, by race, and by sexual preference, all in the name of unity. The schools and colleges that hire and then tenure them commit academic treason. I simply remind you that any intellectual community that is unwilling or unable to identify its enemies cannot defend itself. David Horowitz is exactly right: Those who cherish free institutions, and the culture of wisdom and virtue that sustains them, must stand up boldly against the barbarians already inside the gates.

Because the sixties live, the nineties have become irrational, ignorant, and morally illiterate, as Mortimer Adler, William Bennett, and William Kirk Kilpatrick all recently demonstrated. If the sixties were majestically self-indulgent, the decade of the 1990s is perhaps the most self-congratulatory our nation has ever seen, and not because we have succeeded where all other generations have failed, but in spite of the fact that we have failed where all other American generations have succeeded—in learning to learn, in learning to work, in learning to listen, and in learning to worship. It is a decade determined to ignore, if not belittle and malign, beauty, truth, and goodness, three things most moderns foolishly believe are in the eye of the beholder. The nineties are the sworn enemy of revelation and of righteousness. If the threefold mantra of the sixties was "tune in, turn on, and drop out," that of the nineties is comprised of that earlier mantra's four silly children, four sentences that no thinking man ever permits himself to utter in the face of a moral challenge: "Everything is relative," "There is no right or wrong," "There are no absolutes," and "Who's to say?"

If you cannot now figure out why belief in those four sentences is the death of learning and of virtue, then perhaps for that very reason you can understand why I spend nearly all my time and energy as a professor and as a writer defending the ancient liturgy of the enlightened mind—that right and wrong are matters of fact, not matters of feeling; that without God there is no good; that justice is not equality; that new is not necessarily better; and that relativism, secularism, and pragmatism are not the friends of truth and goodness. The denizens of modernity probably do not realize and probably do not care that they are the befuddled and bedeviled lackeys of designer truth, of made-to-order reality, and of ad hoc morals making. If you follow them, you walk into the night without a light and into the woods without a compass. I want to tell you as plainly as I can that their vision of academic tolerance lacks intellectual virtue. It dilutes the high cultural inheritance of the past with the petty and insupportable leftisms of the present.

A moment ago, I imagined a young person that might be wondering about the relevance of my semi-autobiographical musings. I also can imagine someone thinking that all I've done since the sixties is simply to change sides in the culture war that rages around us. To think so, however, is to assume that flower power and Christianity are morally equivalent and that hippies rank equally with saints, two false assumptions which, if you make them, show just how much a child of the sixties you really are.

I have often wondered why the nineties feel like a sixties renaissance. I discovered the answer to that question in a college cafeteria and in conversations with some of my students' parents.

First, the parents. I have often noticed my students saying and thinking the same sorts of things their parents say and think when I speak with them. Such things happen because the acorn seldom falls far from the oak tree. That fact is significant because the parents of today's college students were probably the young men and women of the sixties. Many of the responses my students learned to give to life are responses they learned from their parents. More often than not, those responses are the stock responses of the sixties. In one way, of course, that's good; I want my students to learn all the truth they can from their parents. But insofar as my students' responses mimic the responses of the sixties, they too must learn the lessons I had to learn. They too must come to understand, with all the clarity and courage they can muster, the truth of the tragic vision of life: We are, every one of us, morally defective, ethically twisted, and spiritually broken. If my students fail to come to that realization and to act upon it, both they and their world shall suffer.

Second, the cafeteria. I often notice my students echoing some of the things they hear their teachers say. When talking with students in the cafeteria, for example, I sometimes have the eerie feeling that I'm not in the cafeteria at all; I'm in a faculty meeting. I say so because I frequently hear the clear and unmistakable intonations of my colleagues' voices, but coming from other people. Sometimes I even hear my own voice. Again, that's good; I want college students to learn all the truth they can from their professors. But here's the rub: Like me, many of their teachers were children of the sixties; and like me, many of those professors have made only an incomplete break with the mistakes of that era. From their other professors and from me, my students have gotten many of their ideas. Like my students themselves, their ideas have parents. Worldviews and attitudes, just like the people who have them, show marked family resemblances. For that very reason, I often want to ask my students this question: From where do you imagine your rampant relativism and your not-very-carefully-hidden contempt for authority arise? In most cases, when I consider asking such a question, I already know the answer—from the sixties and from the people (like me) who reached their emotional and intellectual maturity at that time.

III. Undeception *Redivivus?*

Here's my point: If you believe in the sixties, or if you believe in the nineties, you believe a lie. As I did, you need an undeception. In order to get it, you need to go back well beyond the sixties, back to a wisdom that is older than time. You need to go back to God and to the wisdom that spoke this universe into existence. You need to go back to the God who made you and redeemed you. Real answers are found nowhere else.

It should not surprise you when I tell you that, if you do what I suggest, you'll meet energetic and determined opposition, sometimes even from those who call themselves the friends of God and of tradition. As Socrates observed long centuries ago, most men do not take kindly to the preacher of moral reform, to the pursuer of the good. There's just no telling, he said in the *Gorgias,* what might happen to such a man. But don't let that stop you. Do it anyway. Do it because you need it; do it because it's right; and do it because it ought to be done. Your task will be difficult. It's always easy to be a modernist; it's always easy to go with the spirit of the age. But in the face of the world's downward slide you must be vigilant, strong, perceptive, and courageous. The world needs people like that, people unafraid to turn around and walk back into the light. Our world needs people like that more now than perhaps it ever has because, everywhere you look, the adversary culture of the sixties has become the dominant culture of the nineties.

Our cultural patrimony is being embezzled from under our very noses. If you think of yourself as a Christian, or as a conservative, or as both, the view from here is haunting: We don't own the White House; we don't own the courts; we don't own the media; we don't own the arts; we don't own the sciences; we don't own the marketplace; we don't own the academy; we don't own anything. We don't even own the Church. It's all owned by the sixties.

Therefore, if, as I did, you find yourself an unwilling or unwitting child of the sixties, I invite you, I exhort you, to turn with an open mind and an open heart to the prophets and apostles in Scripture and to the great poets and sages outside Scripture. They are your only liberation from modernist thralldom and from slavery to your own fallen desires. Put yourself on a quest for eternal truth, and never give up until you find Him.

While you're on this quest, you must always remember that most of the powers-that-be are of no help to you. Those who loved the sixties own the nineties. The left still hates America, and it still hates what made America possible: faith in God, individual responsibility, local and limited government, traditional morality, and the sacredness and inviolability of life and of the family. The leftists of the nineties are the enemies of heartland values. They want you to keep quiet. They want you to sit meekly in the corner of the room, hands folded and mouth shut. They want you to be "nice." They want the friends of beauty, truth, and goodness to speak only when spoken to and, when they do speak, to speak only those things that offend no one. That they have offended you seems not to matter. They want you to stick to the script. They want you to keep your views to yourself and to act as if your views were not true, indeed as if there were no truth. That's what political correctness—or should I say political cleansing?—is all about.

Consider it for just a moment: What kind of man or woman would you be if you let yourself be controlled by the empty criticisms of the rootless left, and what kind of world would you be creating for those who came after you if you neglected to restore realism to human thought and turned your back on the only thing that can make you content even in dungeons, even in slums, even in the face of death?

My desire for you is that you throw off the vestiges of leftist cultural subversion, that you make yourself a devotee and guardian of the wisdom of the ages, that you become the sworn enemy of nonsense in all its forms, and, most importantly, that you become the faithful and ardent friend of God. Then, and only then, can you be free.

What has been given you as a heritage you must now accept as your quest. If you wish to be wise, you must learn to learn from your ancestors. You must learn to make peace with the wisdom of the ages and with those who gave it, regardless of their sex, their race, or their ethnic background. You must do so because wisdom and truth are not gender-based, not race-based, and not nation-based. They are thought-based, and thinking is very hard work. Knowledge is not parochial. It is not the private property of any race, any gender, any era, or any ethnic group. It belongs to those determined to get it, to those who seek it resolutely and who will not be denied, no matter how difficult the circmstances arrayed against them. Truth belongs to the diligent and the insightful, and to them only.

In that light, I invite you today to make one of the most important choices of your entire life: Which will you have, truth or rest?

You cannot have both.

The Moral Foundations of Society

Margaret Thatcher

Margaret Thatcher was born in 1925 and went on to earn a degree in chemistry from Somerville College, Oxford, as well as a master of arts degree from the University of Oxford. For some years she worked as a research chemist and then as a barrister, specializing in tax law. Elected to the House of Commons in 1953, she later held several ministerial appointments. She was elected leader of the Conservative Party and thus leader of the Opposition in 1975.

She became Britain's first female prime minister in 1979 and served her nation in this historic role until her resignation in 1990. In 1992, she was elevated to the House of Lords to become Baroness Thatcher of Kesteven. The first volume of her memoirs, *The Downing Street Years,* was published in 1993 by HarperCollins.

The Moral Foundations of the American Founding

History has taught us that freedom cannot long survive unless it is based on moral foundations. The American founding bears ample witness to this fact. America has become the most powerful nation in history, yet she uses her power not for territorial expansion but to perpetuate freedom and justice throughout the world.

For over two centuries, Americans have held fast to their belief in freedom for all men—a belief that springs from their spiritual heritage. John Adams, second president of the United States, wrote in 1789, "Our Constitution was designed only for a moral and religious people. It is wholly inadequate for the government of any other." That was an astonishing thing to say, but it was true.

15

What kind of people built America and thus prompted Adams to make such a statement? Sadly, too many people, especially young people, have a hard time answering that question. They know little of their own history. (This is also true in Great Britain.) But America's is a very distinguished history, nonetheless, and it has important lessons to teach us regarding the necessity of moral foundations.

John Winthrop, who led the Great Migration to America in the early 17th century and who helped found the Massachusetts Bay Colony, declared, "We shall be as a City upon a Hill." On the voyage to the New World, he told the members of his company that they must rise to their responsibilities and learn to live as God intended men should live: in charity, love, and cooperation with one another. Most of the early colonists were infused with the same spirit, and they tried to live in accord with a Biblical ethic. They felt they weren't able to do so in Great Britain or elsewhere in Europe. Some of them were Protestant, and some were Catholic; it didn't matter. What mattered was that they did not feel they had the liberty to worship freely and, therefore, to live freely, at home. With enormous courage, the first American colonists set out on a perilous journey to an unknown land—without government subsidies and not in order to amass fortunes but to fulfill their faith.

Christianity is based on the belief in a single God as evolved from Judaism. Most important of all, the faith of America's founders affirmed the sanctity of each individual. Every human life—man or woman, child or adult, commoner or aristocrat, rich or poor—was equal in the eyes of the Lord. It also affirmed the responsibility of each individual.

This was not a faith that allowed people to do whatever they wished, regardless of the consequences. The Ten Commandments, the injunction of Moses ("Look after your neighbor as yourself"), the Sermon on the Mount, and the Golden Rule made Americans feel precious—and also accountable—for the way in which they used their God-given talents. Thus they shared a deep sense of obligation to one another. And, as the years passed, they not only formed strong communities but devised laws that would protect individual freedom—laws that would eventually be enshrined in the Declaration of Independence and the U.S. Constitution.

Freedom with Responsibility

Great Britain, which shares much of her history in common with America, has also derived strength from its moral foundations, especially since the 18th century when freedom gradually began to spread throughout her society. Many people were greatly influenced by the sermons of John Wesley (1703–1791), who took the Biblical ethic to the people in a way which the institutional church itself had not done previously.

But we in the West must also recognize our debt to other cultures. In the pre-Christian era, for example, the ancient philosophers like Plato and Aristotle had much to contribute to our understanding of such concepts as truth, goodness, and virtue. They knew full well that responsibility was the price of freedom. Yet it is doubtful whether truth, goodness, and virtue founded on reason alone would have endured in the same way as they did in the West, where they were based upon a Biblical ethic.

Sir Edward Gibbon (1737–1794), author of *The Decline and Fall of the Roman Empire,* wrote tellingly of the collapse of Athens, which was the birthplace of democracy. He judged that, in the end, more than they wanted freedom, the Athenians wanted security. Yet they lost everything—security, comfort, and freedom. This was because they wanted not to give to society, but for society to give to them. The freedom they were seeking was freedom from responsibility. It is no wonder, then, that they ceased to be free. In the modern world, we should recall the Athenians' dire fate whenever we confront demands for increased state paternalism.

To cite a more recent lesson in the importance of moral foundations, we should listen to Czech President Vaclav Havel, who suffered grievously for speaking up for freedom when his nation was still under the thumb of communism. He has observed, "In everyone there is some longing for humanity's rightful dignity, for moral integrity, and for a sense that transcends the world of existence." His words suggest that in spite of all the dread terrors of communism, it could not crush the religious fervor of the peoples of Eastern Europe and the Soviet Union.

So long as freedom, that is, freedom with responsibility, is grounded in morality and religion, it will last far longer than the kind that is grounded only in abstract, philosophical notions. Of course, many foes of morality and religion have attempted to argue that new scientific discoveries make belief in God obsolete, but what they actually demonstrate is the remarkable and unique nature of man and the universe. It is hard not to believe that these gifts were given by a divine Creator, who alone can unlock the secrets of existence.

Societies Without Moral Foundations

The most important problems we have to tackle today are problems, ultimately, having to do with the moral foundations of society. There are people who eagerly accept their own freedom but do not respect the freedom of others—they, like the Athenians, want freedom from responsibility. But if they accept freedom for themselves, they must respect the freedom of others. If they expect to go about their business unhindered and to be protected from violence, they must not hinder the business of or do violence to others.

They would do well to look at what has happened in societies without moral foundations. Accepting no laws but the laws of force, these societies have been ruled by totalitarian ideologies like Nazism, fascism, and communism, which do not spring from the general populace but are imposed on it by intellectual elites.

It was two members of such an elite, Marx and Lenin, who conceived of "dialectical materialism," the basic doctrine of communism. It robs people of all freedom—from freedom of worship to freedom of ownership. Marx and Lenin desired to substitute their will not only for all individual will but for God's will. They wanted to plan everything; in short, they wanted to become gods. Theirs was a breathtakingly arrogant creed, and it denied above all else the sanctity of human life.

The 19th-century French economist and philosopher Frederic Bastiat once warned against this creed. He questioned those who, "though they are made of the same human clay as the rest of us, think they can take away all our freedoms and exercise them on our behalf." He would have been appalled but not surprised that the communists of the 20th century took away the freedom of millions of individuals, starting with the freedom to worship. The communists viewed religion as "the opiate of the people." They seized Bibles as well as all other private property at gun point and murdered at least 10 million souls in the process. Thus 20th-century Russia entered into the greatest experiment in government and atheism the world had ever seen, just as America several centuries earlier had entered into the world's greatest experiment in freedom and faith.

Communism denied all that the Judeo-Christian tradition taught about individual worth, human dignity, and moral responsibility. It was not surprising that it collapsed after a relatively brief existence. It could not survive more than a few generations because it denied human nature, which is fundamentally moral and spiritual. (It is true that no one predicted the collapse would come so quickly and so easily. In retrospect, we know that this was due in large measure to the firmness of President Ronald Reagan who said, in effect, to Soviet leader Mikhail Gorbachev, "Do not try to beat us militarily, and do not think that you can extend your creed to the rest of the world by force.")

The West began to fight the moral battle against communism in earnest in the 1980s, and it was our resolve—combined with the spiritual strength of the people suffering under the system who finally said, "Enough!"—that helped restore freedom in Eastern Europe and the Soviet Union—the freedom to worship, speak, associate, vote, establish political parties, start businesses, own property, and much more. If communism had been a creed with moral foundations, it might have survived, but it was not, and it simply could not sustain itself in a world that had such shining examples of freedom, namely, America and Great Britain.

The Moral Foundations of Capitalism

It is important to understand that the moral foundations of a society do not extend only to its political system; they must extend to its economic system as well. America's commitment to capitalism is unquestionably the best example of this principle. Capitalism is not, contrary to what those on the left have tried to argue, an amoral system based on selfishness, greed, and exploitation. It is a moral system based on a Biblical ethic. There is no other comparable system that has raised the standard of living of millions of people, created vast new wealth and resources, or inspired so many beneficial innovations and technologies.

The wonderful thing about capitalism is that it does not discriminate against the poor, as has been so often charged; indeed, it is the only economic system that raises the poor out of poverty. Capitalism also allows nations that are not rich in natural resources to prosper. If resources were the key to wealth, the richest country in the world would be Russia, because it has abundant supplies of everything from oil, gas, platinum, gold, silver, aluminum, and copper to timber, water, wildlife, and fertile soil.

Why isn't Russia the wealthiest country in the world? Why aren't other resource-rich countries in the Third World at the top of the list? It is because their governments deny citizens the liberty to use their God-given talents. Man's greatest resource is himself, but he must be free to use that resource.

In his recent encyclical, *Centesimus Annus,* Pope John Paul II addressed this issue. He wrote that the collapse of communism is not merely to be considered as a "technical problem." It is a consequence of the violation of human rights. He specifically referred to such human rights as the right to private initiative, to own property, and to act in the marketplace. Remember the "Parable of the Talents" in the New Testament? Christ exhorts us to be the best we can be by developing our skills and abilities, by succeeding in all our tasks and endeavors. What better description can there be of capitalism? In creating new products, new services, and new jobs, we create a vibrant community of work. And that community of work serves as the basis of peace and goodwill among all men.

The Pope also acknowledged that capitalism encourages important virtues, like diligence, industriousness, prudence, reliability, fidelity, conscientiousness, and a tendency to save in order to invest in the future. It is not material goods but all of these great virtues, exhibited by individuals working together, that constitute what we call the "marketplace."

The Moral Foundations of the Law

Freedom, whether it is the freedom of the marketplace or any other kind, must exist within the framework of law. Otherwise it means only freedom for the strong to oppress the weak. Whenever I visit the former Soviet Union, I stress this point with students, scholars, politicians, and businessmen—in short, with everyone I meet. Over and over again, I repeat: Freedom must be informed by the principle of justice in order to make it work between people. A system of laws based on solid moral foundations must regulate the entire life of a nation.

But this is an extremely difficult point to get across to people with little or no experience with laws except those based on force. The concept of justice is entirely foreign to communism. So, too, is the concept of equality. For over seventy years, Eastern Europe and the Soviet Union had no system of common law. There were only the arbitrary and often contradictory dictates of the Communist Party. There was no independent judiciary. There was no such thing as truth in the communist system.

And what is freedom without truth? I have been a scientist, a lawyer, and a politician, and from my own experience I can testify that it is nothing. The third-century Roman jurist Julius Paulus said, "What is right is not derived from the rule, but the rule arises from our knowledge of what is right." In other words, the law is founded on what we believe to be true and just. It has moral foundations. Once again, it is important to note that the free societies of America and Great Britain derive such foundations from a Biblical ethic.

The Moral Foundations of Democracy

Democracy is never mentioned in the Bible. When people are gathered together, whether as families, communities or nations, their purpose is not to ascertain the will of the majority, but the will of the Holy Spirit. Nevertheless, I am an enthusiast of democracy because it is about more than the will of the majority. If it were only about the will of the majority, it would be the right of the majority to oppress the minority. The American Declaration of Independence and Constitution make it clear that this is not the case. There are certain rights which are human rights and which no government can displace. And when it comes to how you Americans exercise your rights under democracy, your hearts seem to be touched by something greater than yourselves. Your role in democracy does not end when you cast your vote in an election. It applies daily; the standards and values that are the moral foundations of society are also the foundations of your lives.

Democracy is essential to preserving freedom. As Lord Acton reminded us, "Power tends to corrupt, and absolute power corrupts absolutely." If no individual can be trusted with power indefinitely, it is even more true that no government can be. It has to be checked, and the best way of doing so is through the will of the majority, bearing in mind that this will can never be a substitute for individual human rights.

I am often asked whether I think there will be a single international democracy, known as a "new world order." Though many of us may yearn for one, I do not believe it will ever arrive. We are misleading ourselves about human nature when we say, "Surely we're too civilized, too reasonable, ever to go to war again," or, "We can rely on our governments to get together and reconcile our differences." Tyrants are not moved by idealism. They are moved by naked ambition. Idealism did not stop Hitler; it did not stop Stalin. Our best hope as sovereign nations is to maintain strong defenses. Indeed, that has been one of the most important moral as well as geopolitical lessons of the 20th century. Dictators are encouraged by weakness; they are stopped by strength. By strength, of course, I do not merely mean military might but the resolve to use that might against evil.

The West did show sufficient resolve against Iraq during the Persian Gulf War. But we failed bitterly in Bosnia. In this case, instead of showing resolve, we preferred "diplomacy" and "consensus." As a result, a quarter of a million people were massacred. This was a horror that I, for one, never expected to see again in my lifetime. But it happened. Who knows what tragedies the future holds if we do not learn from the repeated lessons of history? The price of freedom is still, and always will be, eternal vigilance.

Free societies demand more care and devotion than any others. They are, moreover, the only societies with moral foundations, and those foundations are evident in their political, economic, legal, cultural, and, most importantly, spiritual life.

We who are living in the West today are fortunate. Freedom has been bequeathed to us. We have not had to carve it out of nothing; we have not had to pay for it with our lives. Others before us have done so. But it would be a grave mistake to think that freedom requires nothing of us. Each of us has to earn freedom anew in order to possess it. We do so not just for our own sake, but for the sake of our children, so that they may build a better future that will sustain over the wider world the responsibilities and blessings of freedom.

This Unique Moment

David F. Wells

David F. Wells, an ordained Congregational minister, is the Andrew Mutch Distinguished Professor of Historical and Systematic Theology at Gordon-Conwell Theological Seminary in Massachusetts. Born in Bulawayo, Southern Rhodesia (now Zimbabwe), he studied at the University of Capetown and became a professional architect in England. In the 1960s, he returned to school, earning degrees in theology at London University, Trinity Evangelical Divinity School in Deerfield, Illinois, and the University of Manchester.

Dr. Wells began teaching at Trinity Divinity School in 1969 and served as a department and division chairman. He joined the faculty at Gordon-Conwell full time in 1979. He is the author of six books, including: *God in the Wasteland: The Reality of Truth in a World of Fading Dreams, No Place for Truth, or Whatever Happened to Evangelical Theology?, The Person of Christ: A Biblical and Historical Analysis of the Incarnation,* and *The Search for Salvation.* He is also the editor of numerous works, including Eerdmans' *Handbook to Christianity in America.* He devotes much of his spare time to helping provide theological education for leaders and basic preaching tools for pastors in underdeveloped nations.

We are living, I believe, at a unique cultural moment.

Every generation, I know, imagines that it is unique. And most generations, unfortunately, believe that their uniqueness lies in their superiority over all that lies in the past. Mark Twain once observed that when he was a boy, he was embarrassed by his father, who appeared to know so little, but when the younger Twain was a few years older he was amazed at how much his father had learned in so short a period of time! Every generation tries to get airborne on the plastic wings of this kind of conceit, and in this atmosphere it is almost inevitable that we become breathless about the present and begin to say and do foolish things, like the pastor whose morning prayer in church began: "O Lord, have you seen the *New York Times* today?"

I nevertheless believe this is a unique cultural moment. First, I want to lay out my reasons for saying this. Second, I want to elaborate on some of the consequences of this fact for the Church. Third, I want to underline what, in a Christian context, needs to be done next.

A New World Culture

I believe this moment is culturally unique for two reasons.

First, this is the first time that we have seen emerging a *world culture*. There have always been those who have nurtured dreams of global domination, like Napoleon and Hitler, but that is not what I have in mind. I am speaking instead of the emergence of a culture, voluntarily brought about, that looks about the same whether it is encountered in Boston or Paris, London or Bombay, Sydney or Cairo.

What is different about this current condition is that up until now cultures have always been *local* and never global. That is, what any society comes to think of as being normal in matters of belief or behavior has always been determined by that people's history, its traditions, certainly its religion, its ethnicity, and perhaps its geography. Thus it is that we differentiate Russian culture from Indian, African culture from European, Hispanic from Chinese. Cultures have been local, but today we are seeing the birth of a culture that owes little or nothing to anyone in particular and therefore can belong to everyone in general. However, to stretch so far, to incorporate so many otherwise diverse people in its embrace, modern culture must necessarily be very thin, no more than skin deep. It must be stripped of the values which actually give depth and meaning to life.

The reason this is happening now is, of course, that this culture, this world cliché culture, is being constructed by realities which are not localized and whose effects are generic. They are: urbanization, capitalism, technology, and telecommunications. Let me briefly explore these four makers of our modern world.

Urbanization

There have always been cities, but what is different about our time is both the percentage of people who live in a city and the size of our cities. A century ago in America, only 25 percent of the population lived in a city; today 94 percent of the population does. We have moved from being a rural to an urban culture. Throughout the world we are seeing large cities emerge because in the last fifty years the world has doubled in size, and much of this growth has spilled into cities. Today, there are more than four hundred cities with populations of more than one million.

This change in our social organization has had profound effects on how we experience life. Cities bring into close contact those of differing worldviews, religions, and social practices and that means that they enforce a civility, a kind of secular ecumenism that easily breaks down into relativism. The public environment in the city is also impersonal and works by rules that often are not ethically derived but are commercially driven. Urban culture tends to sever our two worlds—that which is private from that which is public—and allows us to live by different values in our different worlds. This bifurcation between private and public as well as the relativism that is so much a part of urban society have profoundly changed what Christian faith means for many people. It has become a largely private matter, its significance is severed from the public square, and its uniqueness as truth is dying. Of those who claim to be evangelical, 40 percent think that other religions are also paths to God and 53 percent think that there are no moral absolutes.

Capitalism

Capitalism is simply the most effective way to produce the goods and services we have come to desire. During the last century in America, industrial output has increased about 5000 percent, in the process generating complex financial, legal, and commercial systems which together have changed the way in which we experience the world. It is the sheer success, the extravagance of our productivity, that has also rewritten our lives around the habits of consuming. Now it is not only products that we consume, but also images, sex, religion, and people, each of which we use if it were a product in order to satisfy an internal need which we, the consumers, have identified.

Technology

Technology is not only transforming our world, and transforming what we can do in the world, but it, too, also transforms the way we experience our world. It was Jacques Ellul who first made the observation that technology tends to create a naturalistic world, one in which we are its sovereigns, over which we preside, where what is efficient becomes what is ethical, and where all problems are resolved by management, not only in the business world but also in the human spirit as well. Today, the two most admired cultural types in our society, Robert Bellah has found, are the manager and the psychologist, and it is not difficult to see, even in the Christian ministry, how intrusive this mentality has become. In the study, the pastor has often become the C.E.O. and in the pulpit a psychologist.

Telecommunications

Television is not only our window upon the world but also our eyes in the world, making us witnesses of all the world's great shaking and shaping events. Television and jet travel together have annihilated space bringing us ever closer to being omnipresent and omniscient, attributes which rest very uneasily on our frail, broken psyches. Space and geographical locale were once the barriers around the human spirit, perhaps producing a narrow ignorance about the world, perhaps unhealthy parochialism, but also a sense of community, securing the many ligaments of human relating which are now gone. Cognitively, we are world citizens, and we scarcely belong in local communities at all.

These are no small developments. Long ago, Reinhold Niehbuhr suggested that the self builds its substance from a threefold connection: to family, community, and craft. What has happened to these? Since 1970, there has been a 200 percent increase in single parent homes and less than 60 percent of children now live with their biological parents. The upshot, for many, has been a loss of connection to family. Modernization has mowed down most geographical communities in America, replacing them with cities and the larger world which we inhabit by television, thus severing another connection. And work is not satisfying for many, either because of its boring, repetitive nature, or because it is encased in a bureaucratic straight jacket. Indeed, 50 percent say that work does not repay in satisfaction what is commensurate with the effort required and thus the third connection is endangered.

It is, I believe, this loss of connectedness to family, community, and work that is driving the anxious search for the self, for self-fulfillment, in our society because all of reality must now be relocated from the exterior world to the internal. Ours, in consequence, is a therapeutic society where all of life's problems are submitted to psychological understanding on the assumption that what were once sins needing forgiveness are now problems needing management, where victimhood is ubiquitous and moral culture is vanishing.

The New Secular Society

This, then, is the culture which is enveloping us, driven by urbanization, capitalism, technology, and telecommunications, and the environment which results is producing a situation unlike any which the Church has faced before. There is, however, a second reason for saying that this is a unique cultural moment.

This is the first time that any major civilization has deliberately attempted to build itself without religious foundations. Beneath other civilizations there have always been such foundations, whether they came from Islam, Hinduism, or Christianity itself. Beneath ours there are none. We are building a civilization of the most marvelous intricacy and complexity, but we are building it upon a vacuum, one in which the processes of life have no framework of ultimacy, one in which they all must find within themselves the reasons for their legitimacy in society. This is not to say that religion has disappeared. Rather, God has been evacuated from the center of our collective life, pushed to the edges of our public square to become an irrelevance to how our world does its business. Marxism rested upon a theoretical theism; our secularized world rests upon a *practical* atheism in the public domain, though one which often coexists with religiosity of various kinds in the private. And this, many say, is what the framers of the Constitution had in mind!

This challenge is not entirely novel. Those who have lived under Marxist regimes recognize some of the elements. What is different, however, is the fact that this practicing atheism goes hand in hand with profession of freedom and is the cultural context in which capitalism is flourishing, filling our world with manifold abundance. This is where the novelty of the challenge lies. The extraordinary and dazzling benefits of our modernized world—benefits that are now indispensable to our way of life—often hide the values which accompany them, values which have the power to wrench around our lives in very damaging ways. It is this matter which we must now take up.

If this is our world, the modernized world in which we now live, is it surprising to learn that most people in America dismiss the idea that there is such a thing as absolute truth? In consequence, according to some polls, 50 percent think that everything in life is up for negotiation, from values to behavior, belief to practice, and 60 percent rest this negotiation on the premise that they can know nothing beyond what they can experience. A majority, 66 percent, do not believe in moral absolutes. It is, however, what lies beneath these figures that we need to explore.

If modernization has often severed connections to family, community, and craft, it has also created a cultural environment in which God has disappeared. This does not mean, however, that everyone in America is blatantly irreligious. As a matter of fact, more people attend church today than they did in Puritan times and non-Christian religions, such as the New Age movement, are growing rapidly. No, what has been lost is not the belief in God in general but the belief in the biblical God, in particular, the God whose nature is centrally defined by His holiness, Who is outside of ourselves, and Who addresses us by His Word, calling us to repentance, faith in Christ, and obedience. This is the God no longer at home in the modern world, and the Church is rapidly accommodating itself to His absence. The telltale signs are everywhere.

The habits and appetites modernity encourages are, today, simply at odds with those that biblical faith requires, and where that has not been recognized a fateful series of substitutions takes place. Faith that has been infused by the spirit of modernity becomes self-focused rather than God-focused. It imagines that the world can be understood aright by gazing through the peephole of the self, so this kind of faith will lean much on intuition and little on God's revealed truth. It will be guided more by circumstance than by conviction, and it will be more pragmatic than principled. Christian faith, in consequence, will be cast in therapeutic terms. Self-fascination replaces the older self-denial, the latter becoming a new obscenity and the former a new gospel. The search for wholeness then replaces that of holiness, feeling good that of being good. This, in turn, begins to obscure the difference between good and evil, or to make that difference one of small consequence, and perhaps out of this there develops an entirely new understanding of what good and evil really are. Good, in a secularized and affluent age, is to have and to have is to be; evil, by the same token, is to be deprived and to be without is to be lost. Salvation, therefore, is not salvation from the judgment of God but simply salvation from the judgment of modernity. To be saved is simply to have a personal sense of well-being, however that comes about. In short, to paraphrase an old saying about dining with the Devil, those who wish to sup with modernity had better have a long spoon because it has the power to wreck faith and to rob us of our ability to think of God's world on God's terms.

The New Counterculture

However, one of the strange new twists in our culture is that modernity has brought forth, from its own loins, its most vociferous critics. I refer to the post-modern artists, authors, rock stars, and movie makers. Inasmuch as they are still a part of what is the modern world, they might better be called anti-modernists than post-modernists, for they have set themselves to attack the soul of modernity.

The world that brought about urbanization, capitalism, technology and telecommunications, it just so happened, also provided an environment that gave great plausibility to En-lightenment ideas. This is why modernity has been so powerful and intrusive. The social context reinforced the ideology, the ideology gave life to the context as soul does to body. Thus it was, for example, that the Enlightenment dismissed all previous sources of religious authority, such as the Church or the Bible, and substituted for them the human being as the source of morality, mystery, and meaning. By an entirely different route, however, modernization has brought us to the same point by severing the connections of the self in family, community, and craft, thus forcing us to relocate all reality from the exterior world to that which is interior. So it was that the Self movement arose and thus it is that we imagine that the art in life is to find the Self and fulfill it. By two entirely different routes we have arrived at the same place: The human being is the source of morality, meaning, mystery, and satisfaction.

What has now happened, however, is that the post-mod-ernists have turned on the Enlightenment, rightly seeing it as a failed project. The attack has been savage. The intellectual soul of modernity has been eviscerated and replaced by empti-ness. Where the Enlightenment spoke of purpose, the post-modernists now have havoc; where the Enlightenment be-lieved that what was true could be rationally discovered, the post-modernists mock the notion of truth as simple nostalgia for the past and believe that reason points to nothing but itself; where the Enlightenment gave itself hope in the thought that life was progressing, the post-modernists have abandoned that hope and plunged into nihilism; and where the Enlighten-ment had order, the post-modernists have only anarchy. They have, in other words, stripped modernity of the hope and sense of order which, however fraudulent they were, had made life a little more bearable.

Enlightenment skeptics attacked Christian faith because, they said, it was not true; post-modern skeptics attack Christian faith because it claims to be true. Thus it is that the battle lines have shifted. Along the way, however, the post-modernists have taught the Christians a lesson. They undertook to deconstruct the Enlightenment worldview simply because it rested upon straws; but we need to deconstruct the modern worldview because it is also sinful. It is, in fact, our own realization of what the Bible speaks of under the language of "the world." Worldliness has very little to do with the trivial taboos with which it is often associated. In the Bible, it is that system of values which takes root in any society that has the fallen human being as its source and center, that relegates God to the margins, and that makes sin look normal and righteousness look strange. Modernity and post-modernity are in large measure for us the world. It is not only from our fallenness, not only from the powers of evil that we are redeemed, but also from the world (Eph. 2:2). Thus it is that God and the world are in competition for our lives. We cannot love the one unless we hate the other (Jas. 4:4).

The chief reason that modernity has been able to toy with the life of the Church as it has is that the Church has not recognized modernized culture for what it is. Most Christians, as a matter of fact, see this culture as essentially neutral and harmless. In a study that was carried out in 1993, for example, the views and attitudes of students from seven evangelical seminaries were studied. While 79 percent affirmed that human nature is essentially "perverse and corrupt," very few of these were able to say that they considered culture or the self as perverse and corrupt—though the one is an extension of human nature and the other is a part—and most saw culture as neutral and the self as innocent. In other words, the transition from theological belief to principled practice in the modern world simply is not being made very well. And these are the Church's leaders of tomorrow.

It is, therefore, our cultural naiveté that is betraying us, but this naiveté is really an outcome of our spiritual weakness and confusion. What we need to find afresh, and to find afresh in the center of our lives, is the truth of God's Word, which will shine its light upon our path and upon our modernized world. More than that, we need to find afresh the God of that Word who alone can sustain us in truth, encourage us in hope, and build that kind of moral character without which we are unrecognizable as His children and unable to resist the powerful currents that flow through our society as it now begins to unravel in very serious ways.

A Time to Stand: The Christian Faith and the Coming Conflict of Civilizations*

Os Guinness

Os Guinness is a Senior Fellow of the Trinity Forum, a seminar program for senior executives and political leaders that focuses on the leading ideas of our day in the context of faith. Born during World War II in China, where his parents were medical missionaries, he remained there until 1951 when the communist government forced foreigners to leave. He pursued his undergraduate studies at the University of London and earned a doctorate in the social sciences from the University of Oxford.

His first book, *The Dust of Death,* is a critique of the counterculture. His second, *In Two Minds,* is on the problem of doubt. His third, *The Gravedigger File,* is an examination of the social and cultural forces shaping religion in the late 20th century. He is the coeditor of *Articles of Faith, Articles of Peace* and *No God But God: Breaking with the Idols of Our Age.* His latest book, *The American Hour,* is an analysis of the United States toward the close of the "American Century." Dr. Guinness is also the author of *Dining with the Devil: The Megachurch Movement Flirts with Modernity* and *Fit Bodies, Fat Minds: Why Evangelicals Don't Think.* He is currently at work on another book on the subject of vocation.

The Swedish town of Uppsala is today surrounded by corn fields, but once it was the sea that lapped at its inhabitants' doors. For five thousand years, humans have settled there. In about the eleventh century A.D., the last of the pagan temples was built, and for one hundred years it was only a few yards away from the first of the Christian churches. These institutions repeatedly clashed. Eventually, Christian faith won, and paganism receded. But as the modern tour guides will tell you,

*Author's note: This is a transcription of a speech I delivered for the first time at Hillsdale College. I apologize in advance for any "roughness" or incompleteness.

35

it is the church in Sweden and, indeed, in many nations of the West, that is receding and paganism that is resurgent in the late twentieth century.

Though it is the most nearly universal religion in most parts of the world, the Christian faith has certainly lost significant ground. Some would say that it is all over for the Christian faith. Following Nietzsche's parable of the madman or Matthew Arnold's poem, "Dover Beach," they would say that the Christian faith, clashing with modernity, is receding and dying. There are more than a few church officials who would agree with them. But others insist that the Christian faith is on the verge of winning the world. They would cite recent, powerful evidence in the sub-Sahara, Africa, Eastern Europe, and the former Soviet Union.

I would argue the first group has lost touch with the gospel, and the second has lost sight of modernity. I belong to a third group, the "orthodox" among Protestants and Catholics, that would be described as having "sober confidence." The orthodox are sober because of the immense challenge of modernity—the greatest challenge the church has ever faced—and confident because of the truth, meaning, and power of the Christian gospel. I don't pretend to be neutral on this. I am an Englishman by nationality, a social scientist by training, a follower of Christ by faith, and an Anglican Evangelical by tradition.

Having made these disclaimers, I want to present a series of brief propositions about the Christian faith, the coming conflict of civilizations, and the reawakening I foresee.

Proposition 1: There are three major revolutions that comprise the challenge of modernity. I spoke at the World Congress on Evangelism in Manila a few years ago, and after I had finished speaking on modernity and mission, an elderly missionary came up to me afterwards and said, "I didn't hear what you said, and I couldn't understand everything I heard, but why on earth did they ask a man to speak on maternity?" There is enormous confusion about modernity but it is really no more subtle than the word *maternity*.

Modernity is the spirit and system of our modern world,

and it is produced by the forces of modernization. We often think of the story of human beings in terms of civilizations— Assyrian, Babylonian, Chinese, Indian, Inca, Greek, Roman, Spanish, French, British, American, and so on. Each civilization is, of course, powerful in its own time and powerful in its own region. But modernity is different: It is the most powerful civilization produced by human beings so far and the first that is genuinely global. It is not tied to a continent, religion, conqueror, or single set of ideas. It is based primarily on revolutions of a different sort.

The first of these is capitalism, which, according to different estimates, really began to flourish in the twelfth, fifteenth or eighteenth century. The second is industrialized technology, which began in England in the late 1700s. The third is telecommunications, starting with the invention of the telegraph and the photograph in the 1800s and continuing today with the information superhighway, virtual reality, and the extraordinary conglomerates not only being built, but in information and entertainment.

Now our place in these three revolutions is obvious. If the nineteenth century was "the British century," as it is often called, the twentieth has been, in Henry Luce's words, "the American century." But the challenge of these revolutions is less obvious. Take capitalism, for example. Social scientist Peter Berger is an unashamed proponent of capitalism, yet he says that, following the second Russian revolution of 1989, capitalism now faces its greatest challenge: capitalism. Capitalism's runaway success is undermining the very values that helped to produce it.

Proposition 2: There are three main laboratory experiments in which to observe the interaction of modernity and the world civilizations. After the collapse of the Soviet Union, the big question was, "Who killed communism?" Most people said, "Obviously, democratic freedom and ideals." Others pointed out the vital role of religion—faith and prayer. And then there were those who cited modernity itself: modern media, modern travel, modern communications, and the way they opened up not just traditional societies but totalitarian societies. Sure, there were

still incarnations of Marx, Lenin, and Big Brother like Gorbachev, but they now had American Express cards. And there
were the brave, heroic students in Tianamen Square who were
getting fax messages from southern California.

Modernity helped greatly to undo Marxism, one of its
three great experiments. The first experiment was and still is
Western democratic capitalism, which has arisen from a Jewish
and Christian background and which is flowing with rather
than against the tide of modernity. The second experiment,
totalitarian socialism, is no longer around in the Soviet form,
but its vestiges remain. It is 150 years younger than the first
experiment, and it arises out of a secular rather than a Judeo-
Christian background. It is more ambivalent in its relationship
with modernity. The third experiment is East Asian capitalism
in Japan and the so-called "little dragons," Singapore, Taiwan,
Hong Kong, and Korea. It arises from a Confucian background, but borrows also from Western influences. Like democratic capitalism, East Asian capitalism is also flowing with the
tide of modernity.

From the Judeo-Christian perspective, Confucianism and
the religion of Islam are taking the place of the challenge of
Marxism. As political scientist Samuel Huntington predicts, the
next world war, if it occurs, may be a war between these civilizations.

*Proposition 3: There are three perspectives on history that are
needed to help us to understand what is going on today.* All are
important, but as you look around America today, the most
needed is the most rare. The first is short-range perspective:
concentrating on events and individuals. It is about Plato and
philosophy, da Vinci and the arts, Dante and Shakespeare and
literature, Newton and science, and so on. The second is me-
dium-range perspective: focusing on periods, convergences,
turning points, and ideas. It is about the Renaissance, the Enlightenment, the French Revolution, Romanticism, Modernism, Post-Modernism, and so on. The third is long-range perspective: the reflective past, focusing on continents, centuries
and millenia. This perspective deals with the foundations of

civilizations, with the contours of human life, with the defining features of empires.

And yet in America most people only have a short-range perspective. Two comments illustrate this point. In the 1970s, an American businessman was sitting next to Chou En-lai, the prime minister of China since 1949, at a state banquet. Being very embarrassed and not knowing what to say, he fumbled around for about several minutes and finally ventured a question: "As a Chinese revolutionary, what do you think of the French Revolution in 1789?"

Chou was silent for even longer than he had been before the question was posed. Finally he turned to the businessman and said, "For us Chinese, it is too soon to say." He was undoubtedly teasing, but his comment shows how different is the typical American perspective. Journalist Bill Moyers adds that most Americans are so prone to get information from television that they know everything about the last twenty-four hours, not that much about the last twenty-four years, and next to nothing about the last twenty-four centuries.

Proposition 4: There are three global trends or reactions that are carried around the world by modernity. The first is geopolitical. In one sense, it is a shift from totalitarianism to tribalism. In another sense, it is a shift from globalization, which is still continuing, to localization. One could give various reasons, but this trend is surely behind the tragic rise of the "mini-holacaust"—the humanitarian nightmare, the witches' brew of ancient hatreds that we have seen recently in places like Bosnia and Ruwanda and we have experienced to some extent in our own country. America has its own group grievances, hatred, and tribalism.

The second trend is more philosophical. The shift in the last generation is from "modernism" to "postmodernism." The modernist's absolute faith in reason, science, technology, and humanism has given way to disillusionment, relativism, and cynicism. You see this increasingly in every country in the modern world. Even where the philosophy doesn't quite reach, its consequences are still felt, because of the power of the media and the consumer culture.

The third trend is ethical. We have abandoned a theistic understanding of right and wrong in favor of a therapeutic understanding. "Wrong" is no longer defined as a wrong before God but as a "crime" before the law; today it is a "sickness" or even a "problem of low esteem" according to psychology.

Proposition 5: There are three great cultural revolutions carried within the forces of modernization. One is the graphics revolution, which has led to the triumph of images over words, much trumpeted by thinkers like Camille Paglia. Until recently, most people had few images in their lives apart from nature, and words were predominant. But now, we are bombarded with bumper stickers, billboards, and screen images. Words, by and large, have become accessories to images and have lost their authority under the impact of the graphics revolution.

The second revolution, the information revolution, has given rise to the triumph of information over wisdom and responsibility. Our modern digital processing has given us a kind of technological Tower of Babel. The effect of this "all-at-onceness" as Daniel Boorstein says, is the creation of a new man: "*Homo up to datum.*" But as he concludes, *Homo up to datum* is a dunce, because with all the information flooding over him daily, he has forgotten what to do with it. He has lost touch with wisdom.

The third revolution is the marketing revolution, leading to the triumph of style over substance. In the past, style was always the outward *expression* of the inner character. But today through the triumph of the images in a consumerist form, style is only the surface, and the substance below simply is not considered interesting. In modern America, in fact, style is the only way many individuals—and many firms marketing products—gain any identity at all.

Proposition 6: There are three main pressures exerted on religion by modernity. The debate here has been confusing and controversial. The early readings of the impact of modernity and religion were wrong, but at least they took account of the fact that modernity has had a greater impact on religious belief, than any other externality. One hundred and fifty years after the debate first began, there is a general consensus that there are three main pressures exerted by modernization on religion.

The first pressure is secularization—not to be confused with secularism, which is a philosophy. It is a process by which successive sectors of modern society have been "liberated" from the decisive influence of religious ideas and religious institutions so that in most parts of the world religion is marginalized. In a way, religion becomes Lewis Carroll's famous Cheshire cat: The body disappears but the grin remains.

The second pressure is privatization—not to be confused with the means of undoing nationalization of property and services. Privatization, when it touches religion, is the process by which a cleavage is produced between the public and private spheres of life. It naturally favors the private sphere, since it is the place where individual freedom, fulfillment, and religion flourish. Under this form of privatization, religion is privately engaging and publicly irrelevant.

The third pressure is pluralization, the extraordinary multiplication of options through choice and change through the private sphere, including at the level of worldviews, ideologies, and faith. But with each acceleration of choice and change, nervousness and uncertainty corrode commitment.

Proposition 7: There are three significant revivals stimulated by modernity, which will be ominous ones for the Christian faith. Modernity, I would stress here, is not anti-religious. There are some religions, like Hinduism and the New Age movement, which it finds quite congenial. But it is hostile toward the biblical family of faith, which includes Judaism, Christianity, and the Muslim religion—faiths that demand an integration with the whole of life.

Modernity first reinforces the revival of polytheism—the worship of many gods. For example, there is a clear trend in American society toward worshipping the environment as Mother Earth.

The second revival is of gnosticism, the ancient faith that held that all that is matter is evil and all that is spirit is good, and that salvation comes only from secret knowledge granted to initiates. The new gnosticism is reinforced by the information revolution, which provides access to knowledge in many forms, from hypertext to virtual reality. There is a severe discounting of the body and an esoteric interest in the mind.

The third revival is of paganism, which may be traced through the theraputic revolution and particularly through the rise of Freudian and Jungian psychological theories. The first, Freudian theory, attacks all forms of religion as mania. The second, Jungian theory, is not opposed to religion, but it leads in a very different direction than Christian orthodoxy—toward natural impulses, spiritualism, and the demonic, which are far closer to the new paganism.

Proposition 8: There are three main storm fronts where the brunt of modernity is coming down on the Christian church: Japan, Western Europe and the United States. The state of the gospel on two of these fronts is especially disheartening. Japan has never ever been won to Christ. Western Europe has been won twice to the Christian gospel and lost twice, and the church is not doing very well there today. But it is in the United States that the battle for the Christian faith in the modern world is pivotal.

Why is this so? The first reason is that so much of the meaning of the modern world is wrapped up in the meaning of America. The second reason is that the American church has and is bearing the brunt of the attack against the Christian faith. And the third reason is that the American people have, more than any other people, endured the fiery brook of modernity. Today, there is a third generation that has stood the test of faith. The fourth reason is that America, despite her very real problems, is the strongest nation in the world—spiritually, theologically, numerically, financially, and culturally.

Proposition 9: There are three choices concerning religion in the public square in America. One extreme choice is to argue for a sacred public square, in other words, a public square where one religion or ideology is preferred or semiestablished. Under the conditions of today's pluralism, this choice would be unjust and unworkable. (By the way, it is important to note that this applies to the religion of secularism just as much as it does to any conventional religion.)

The other extreme is the naked public square, where all religions and all ideologies are ostensibly squeezed out. This would be equally unjust and unworkable, mainly because it wouldn't be consistent. One religion or ideology would creep back in. It would also leave the public square with no moral justification. But the pressure for the naked public square comes from two powerful sources. One is those individuals who demand neutrality in public life, for whatever high-minded reason, even though neutrality is impossible. The other source—and it is sometimes comprised of the same individuals—feels revulsion against extremist ways of bringing religion into the public square. These individuals are reacting to some of the unwise ways of the "Religious Right."

The third choice is to create a civil public square, in other words, a public square that is open to citizens of all faiths to enter and engage in public life on the basis of their own commitments and presuppositions, but within constitutional limits and with civility. A respect for truth, other people, and the rights and responsibilities of a common vision for the common good would prevail. Now, as we can see only too clearly during every election year, civility is almost washed away in America today, and it has become for many people a wimp word. But you only need to go to the former Soviet Union or South Africa to realize that civility is a precious commodity.

Proposition 10: There are three choices concerning individual citizens in the public square. The first extreme is the tribesman. He enters public life with no concern for the common good, because of his solidarity and allegiance to his own group. You know, "It's a *black* thing." Or simply substitute for *black* the word *feminist, gay, handicapped, fundamentalist. . . .* Too many Christians as well non-Christians have gone along with this balkanization.

The other extreme is to be an idiot. He is not mentally deficient but, according to the Greek definition of the word, is a person who has a purely private understanding of everything, including the public square. In ancient times, idiots entered and fought for their own interests and ideas, regardless of any influence of others. They were equally careless about the common good but from an individualistic rather than a tribal perspective.

The third option is the citizen, the person who knows well what his interests are, what his agenda is and yet fights not just because of them but because of his deep sense of commitment to the rights and responsibilities of the common vision for the common good.

Proposition 11: There are three stances for believers in relation to modernity. The story of the Christian faith is the story of a two-thousand-year conversation between the church and the world. Christians are called to be in the world, but not of the world, or, as the early church put it, to plunder the Egyptians, but not to set up the Golden Calf. Of course, during the last two millenia, some Christians have gotten too close to the world and compromised, and some have retreated too far from the world and been irrelevant. But modernity has taken those extremes to a new stage; the responses are now more exaggerated and adopting the middle position is harder than ever.

One extreme is to accommodate and finally surrender to the modern world. Many trace this stance in its modern form to Schleiermacher and his attempt to reach the "cultured despisers" of the Gospel. Indeed, much of the story of liberalism has been about ending up too close to the "enemy." This was certainly one of the reasons for the suicide of liberalism and the rise of the "God is dead" movement in the sixties. In other words, a process of accommodation that is uncritical leads to surrender, where there is no remainder, and, finally, you have not the Christian gospel, but another gospel.

The other extreme is defiance, leading to withdrawal and finally to irrelevance in the world. This stance has been seen often in the Jewish ghetto and the Anabaptist subculture, which are totally divorced from the cultures surrounding them. But this stance is becoming harder and harder to maintain because modernity is so powerful and so pervasive.

The third stance is what sociologist Peter Berger calls "bargaining." He who dines with the devil of modernity better have a long spoon. But there are two features to the challenge of bargaining. One is critical discrimination. Without any sense of discrimination or discernment, one cannot pick and choose between things in a way that is mature and wise. The second feature that bargaining requires is constructive transformation. In biblical terms, one must be salt and light. We penetrate through our engagement and slowly transform, producing more truth, more justice, more beauty, more freedom than was there before.

Proposition 12: There are three prevalent deficiencies in American discipleship as it seeks to cope with modernity. The real challenge to religious believers is to maintain their integrity, effectiveness and, above all, the integration of their faith with every part of their lives.

One deficiency was mentioned earlier: privatization. Because of the very shape of modernity, faith becomes privately engaging, publicly irrelevant. In a word, privatization lacks a sense of totality.

The second deficiency is politicization. Many Christians—reacting to privatization by rocketing out of the closet into the culture—define politics as the be-all-and-end-all of their Christian obedience. But if privatization lacks totality because it is restricted to the private sphere, politicization, in a word, lacks tension, the critical tension of being in, but not of the world.

The third deficiency is pillarization. The word goes back to nineteenth-century Holland. The Dutch response to pluralism was to allow all cultures to "do their own thing." There were Protestant and Catholic churches, schools, universities, newspapers, labor unions and so on. The same was true for the humanists, without the churches. The effect was a pillarized nation. It was a much more consistently, coherently, creatively Christian nation, but it lacked, in a word, transformation. There was a tendency to withdraw from society, build up the Christian this-that-and-the-other and no longer engage strategically and penetratingly with Dutch culture. In the end, Holland went "soft," as the saying goes, and was secularized from within. You can see a similar pillarization in America today, with the lure of Anabaptism, the lure of going back to the basics.

Proposition 13: There are three essential requirements to overcoming modernity. The first is transcendence in faith and worship. G.K. Chesterton remarked at the turn of the century that the worldview of the average modern man was like that of a slightly drowsy, middle-aged businessman right after a good lunch. In other words, as Peter Berger put it more prosaically, we live in a world without windows where the ordinary reality has become the only reality and many individuals are atheists unawares, except for the religious language they still use.

I gave some lectures on a different aspect of modernity in Australia a few years ago. A CEO came up to me and he said, "Now I understand something. I was sharing my faith with a Japanese CEO and he said to me, 'I'm not impressed by what I see. Every time I meet a Buddhist monk, I meet a holy man in touch with an unseen world. When I meet a Christian missionary I meet a manager.'" The fact is that in both faith and worship there is a profound loss of transcendence in much of our belief in America.

The second requirement is integration in all our callings. The dualism in the church has a long history, going back to the fourth century when the spiritual was considered higher, and there was a compartment between the spiritual and the secular. The spiritual was the perfect life and the secular was the permitted life. But in the sixteenth century, Martin Luther blew that theory apart. He argued that everyone, everywhere, in everything they did, were as unto God. The Puritans agreed with this and did much to spread Luther's view. But today the notion of dualism has crept back into our society, through privatization and such notions as full-time Christian service and so on. Thus, the central challenge to faith in the modern world is the challenge to integration. Our faith should not just be reserved for church or home but for law school, the CEO's office, the factory floor, and every other inch of life where a disciple goes.

The third requirement is persuasion in our witness and communication. Persuasion has always been at the heart of the

Christian gospel, and at the heart of the expansion of the church through much of its two thousand years. It has also been at the heart of the story of America, particularly as it has faced the challenge of pluralism. But the last two generations have seen the death of persuasion and the rise of a persuasion-less form of faith. It is easy to understand why many of the so-called communications methods or witnessing methods cropped up in the 1940s and 1950s when most people talked Christian and there was no need to persuade. People were open and interested. Today, however, central sectors of society are secularized, and private life is pluralized, and fewer and fewer people speak in Christian terms.

The lack of persuasion is now fatal, and what was once kept at the level of witnessing has now spilled over into politics. Look at the pro-life movement, for example. Loaded terms abound, from "pro-life extremists" on one side and "baby-killers," on the other. There is almost no attempt to persuade hearts and minds, no winning of culture. Yet persuasion in communication is one of the prime needs of the modern world.

Proposition 14: There are three grounds for an unshakable Christian confidence in the face of modernity. I recall a seminar at Oxford in the early 1970s which was highlighted by a discussion between an eminent European sociologist, and an eminent philosopher of Marxism. Both men predicted that Marxism, which was then seriously declining, had no hope for any renewal within itself at all. But they added that the Christian church, with all its faults and problems, had three advantages that made renewal possible.

One advantage was that in the Word of God we have a judgment that transcends history and culture. Though the church has throughout the generations fallen captive—the great metaphor is the Babylonian captivity—it has held on to a great measure of God's truth. And when His Word speaks, it is a Word that transcends history and culture and that awakens even the dead.

The second advantage is, ironically, a belief in sin. Christians have a doctrine of their own failure. At the heart of the gospel is the reality that all of us often go wrong. And while we would like to forget it (and in our pride and arrogance often do), that doctrine is always there to confront us and bring us back to the place where we went wrong in order to repent.

The third advantage is the number of awakenings and revivials among Christians over the last two thousand years. This is particularly true in America, where there are powerful, historic precedents. Indeed, the story of America is virtually the story of awakenings and revivals. It is important to note that they were never purely private. Individual lives were changed, families were changed, schools were changed, neighborhoods were changed, communities were changed, cities were changed. And the effects rippled nationwide. It is no accident that many of today's leading scholars like Irving Kristol and James Q. Wilson argue that it is only through revival that some of the deepest dimensions of our cultural crises can be remedied, or that as G.K. Chesterton put it much more simply a generation ago, "Five times the church has gone to the dogs, but each time it was the dogs that died."

These, I believe, are just some of the elements of the discussion of the Christian faith at the end of the second millenia, which is facing not only the supreme challenge of modernity but the challenge of ancient civilizations themselves being awakened by modernity. This is no time for despair, or complacency, or pessimism, or cynicism. It is a time to stand, and a time to speak, and a time to act. We probably all have our own favorite examples of stands: Elijah's before the prophets of Baal at Mt. Carmel in the Old Testament, Martin Luther at the Wittenburg door or on the second day of the Diet of Worms in 1521, Don John at the Battle of Lopento in 1571, and so on. Let me share with you one that is not a Christian example but is still deeply stirring. It is the stand of Leonidas I, the prince of Sparta in 480 B.C.

Do you know the history of that time? Xerxes, the so-called "king of kings," was the emperor of Persia, and his army was sweeping across the Hellespont to attack Greece. The main target was Athens. But Athens was not yet the shining city of Pericles. It was just a little city that had a genius for annoying empires. And when the Persians flowed through, the Greek league managed to put in its way seven thousand soldiers under the generalship of Leonidas, the prince of Sparta. They faced the biggest army the world had ever seen, far more than 100,000 invaders sweeping down upon them.

They took their position at a place which in English is called "hot gates," the pass of Thermopylae, where five-thousand-foot mountains fall off sharply to almost meet the sea. For four days, Leonidas and his men held the pass and kept the Persians away from Greece. For four days, Xerxes sent his best troops; finally he sent the Immortals, and even they fell back. But, inevitably, a traitor betrayed the Greeks, and they woke up on the fifth day to find themselves surrounded. Leonidas knew what he was facing, and, of the seven thousand, he dismissed all but three hundred, his own Spartans, who were known for fierce fighting, and winning or dying, as it was said. They made their stand on a little mound you can still see today. They fought to the last man, and they died.

But before they died, Leonidas sent back this message to Sparta, "Stranger, tell the Spartans that we have behaved as they would wish us to behave, and we are buried here." Magnificently laconic, understated, and nonmelodramatic, but effective. As he lay dying, Leonidas had no idea that, in the following year, five thousand Spartans would beat the huge army of the Persians. He had no idea that in thirty years the Athens of Pericles, Plato, Aristotle, Sophocles, Euripides, and Aeschylus would have begun to flower. He had no idea that when he stood that day in 480 B.C. on the line of freedom, he was making a difference—a difference that we can truly say affects our freedom all these thousands of years later.

There is no one place we can make a stand today, there is no one enemy. Yet we can and must confront the challenge of modernity, which is really a challenge to the integrity and effectiveness of our faith. We can and must trust only in what we know to be true.

We must make our stand in our own place in time and leave the outcome to God. May it be said of us, as it was said of the Spartans, "Stranger, tell our people that we have behaved as they would wish us to behave, and we are buried here."

The Religious Roots of Freedom

M. Stanton Evans

M. Stanton Evans is chairman of the Education and Research Institute and
director of the National Journalism Center in Washington, D.C. The Center trains young, aspiring reporters and boasts alumni at the *Detroit News,*
the *Wall Street Journal,* the *Washington Post,* CNN, C-SPAN, Evans & Novak,
the Associated Press, plus dozens of journals and newspapers around the
country.

Mr. Evans has also served as managing editor of *Human Events,* associate editor of *National Review,* and editor of the *Indianapolis News.* For many
years a syndicated columnist for the *Los Angeles Times,* he has written seven
books, including: *Revolt on the Campus, The Future of Conservatism: From Taft
to Reagan and Beyond,* and *Clear and Present Dangers: A Conservative's View of
America's Government,* and, most recently, *The Theme Is Freedom.*

Nowhere is the cultural conflict of the modern era more
apparent than in the dispute about the place of religion in the
civic order. Here the battle is overt, relentless, and pervasive—
with traditional belief and custom retreating before a secularist
onslaught in our courts and other public institutions.

During the past three decades, the U.S. Supreme Court
has handed down a series of rulings that decree a "wall of
separation" between affairs of state and the precepts of religion. In the most controverted of these cases, in 1962, the
Court said an officially sponsored prayer recited in the New
York public schools was an abridgement of our freedoms. This

This article is adapted with permission from his book *The Theme Is Freedom: Religion,
Politics, and the American Tradition* (Regnery, 1994) and also appeared in the January
23, 1995 issue of *National Review.*

prayer read, in its entirety: "Almighty God, we acknowledge our dependence on Thee, and we beg Thy blessings upon us, our parents, our teachers, and our country." In the Court's opinion, this supplication triggered the First Amendment ban against an "establishment of religion," logic that was later extended to reading the Bible and reciting the Lord's Prayer in the classroom.

In adopting the First Amendment, according to the Court, the Founders meant to sever all connection between religious faith and government, requiring that religion be a purely private matter. As Justice Hugo Black put it in an oft-quoted statement: "The 'establishment of religion' clause of the First Amendment means at least this: Neither a state nor the federal government can set up a church. Neither can pass laws which aid one religion, aid all religions, or prefer one religion over another. . . . No tax in any amount, large or small, can be levied to support any religious activities or institutions, whatever they may be called, or whatever form they may adopt to teach or practice religion."

This doctrine has been affirmed and amplified in many rulings since. In support of it, Black and his successors (most recently Justice David Souter) have offered a reading of our history that supposedly shows the intentions of the people who devised the First Amendment. In a nutshell, this tells us that the Founders chiefly responsible for the Constitution's religion clauses were Madison and Jefferson; that they held views intensely hostile toward any governmental backing for religion; and that the amendment was a triumph for their separationist position.

Of Whole Cloth

The First Amendment depicted by Justice Black and other liberal jurists is, unfortunately, a fabrication. The Supreme Court's alleged history is a prime example of picking and choosing elements from the past to suit the ideological fashions of the present. If we consult the history of the nation's founding, we find that the Court and its supporters have misstated the material facts about the issue in every possible fashion.

To begin with, state papers, legal arrangements, and political comment of the founding generation show that American culture of that period was suffused with religious doctrine. The point is made, ironically, by the very concept of an "establishment of religion." This term had a definite meaning in England and the colonies that is critical to understanding the debate about the First Amendment. It signified an official church that occupied a privileged position with the state, was vested with certain powers denied to others, and was supported from the public treasury. Such was the Church of England in Great Britain, and such also were numerous churches in the colonies at the beginning of our revolution.

The States' Churches

In 1775, no fewer than nine colonies had such arrangements. Massachusetts, Connecticut, and New Hampshire had systems of local church establishment in favor of the Congregationalists. In the South, from Maryland on down, the establishments were Episcopalian. In New York, there was a system of locally supported Protestant clergy. Because of growing religious diversity within the states, pressure mounted to disestablish these official churches. In particular, increasingly numerous Baptists and Presbyterians made headway against the Anglican position, which was further weakened by the identification of many Episcopal ministers with the English.

Even so, at the time of the Constitutional Convention, the three New England states still had their Congregational establishments. In other states, there remained a network of official sanctions for religious belief, principally the requirement that one profess a certain kind of Christian doctrine to hold public office or enjoy other legal privilege. With local variations, these generally tended in the same direction, and they make instructive reading alongside the statements of Justices Black and Souter about the supposed history of our institutions.

In South Carolina, for example, the Constitution of 1778

said that "the Christian Protestant religion shall be deemed ...
the established religion of the state." It further said that no
religious society could be considered a church unless it agreed
"that there is one eternal God and a future state of rewards and
punishment; that the Christian religion is the true religion;
that the Holy Scriptures of the Old and New Testaments are
of divine inspiration." South Carolina also asserted that "no
person who denies the existence of a Supreme Being shall hold
any office under this Constitution."

Similar statements can be gleaned from other state enact-
ments of the period. The Maryland Constitution of 1776 de-
creed, for instance, "a general and equal tax for the support
of the Christian religion." New Jersey that year expressed its
idea of toleration by saying that "no Protestant inhabitant of
this colony shall be denied the enjoyment of any civil right."
Massachusetts, in 1780, authorized a special levy to support
"public Protestant teachers of piety, religion, and morality"—a
formula adopted verbatim by New Hampshire.

Official support for religious faith and state religious requirements for public office persisted well after adoption of
the First Amendment. The established church of Massachusetts was not abolished until 1833. In New Hampshire, the
requirement that one had to be Protestant to serve in the
legislature was continued until 1877. In New Jersey, Roman
Catholics were not permitted to hold office until 1844. In Maryland, the stipulation that one had to be a Christian lasted until
1826. As late as 1835, one had to be a Protestant to take office
in North Carolina; until 1868, the requirement was that one
had to be a Christian; thereafter that one had to profess a
belief in God.

The official sanction for religious belief provided by the
states was equally apparent at the federal level, during and
after the Revolution. Appeals for divine assistance, days of
prayer and fasting, and other religious observance were common in the Continental Congress. Among its first items of
business, in 1774, the Congress decided to appoint a chaplain
and open its proceedings with a prayer. When it was objected
that this might be a problem because of diversity in religious
doctrine, Sam Adams answered: "I am not a bigot. I can hear

a prayer from a man of piety and virtue, who is at the same time a friend of his country."

On June 12, 1775, the Congress called for "a day of public humiliation, fasting, and prayer," wherein "[we] offer up our joint supplications to the all-wise, omnipotent, and merciful disposer of all events." In observance of this fast day, Congress attended an Anglican service in the morning and a Presbyterian service in the afternoon.

During the Revolutionary War, Congress made provision for military chaplains, recommended that officers and men attend religious service, and threatened court martial for anyone who misbehaved on such occasions. It also adopted the Northwest Ordinance, stressing the need for "religion and morality," appropriated money for the Christian education of Indians, and encouraged the printing of a Bible. The Northwest Ordinance and the measures regarding chaplains, official prayer, and education of the Indians were re-adopted by the first Congress under the new Constitution and maintained for many years thereafter.

Crumbling Wall

Such was the body of doctrine and official practice that surrounded the First Amendment—immediately predating it, adopted while it was being discussed and voted on, and enduring long after it was on the books. The resulting picture is very different from any notion of America as a country run by secularists and Deists. Nor does it look very much like a country in which the governing powers were intent on creating a "wall of separation" between church and state, denying official support to the precepts of religion.

This was the background to Madison's motion on June 8, 1789, introducing a set of amendments to the Constitution, culled from the proposals of conventions. Among the measures that he offered was this pertaining to an establishment of religion: "The civil rights of none shall be abridged on account of religious belief, nor shall any national religion be established...." In view of the weight that has been given to Madison's personal opinions on the subject, his comments on this occasion are of special interest. For example, challenged by Roger Sherman as to why such guarantees were needed, given the doctrine of "enumerated powers," Madison said:

> *he apprehended the meaning of the words to be,* that Congress shall not establish a religion and enforce the legal observation of it by law, nor compel men to worship God in any manner contrary to their conscience. *Whether the words are necessary or not, he did not mean to say, but they had been required by some of the state conventions, who seemed to entertain an opinion that* [under the "necessary and proper" clause] ... Congress ... might infringe the rights of conscience and establish a national religion; to prevent these effects *he presumed the amendment was intended,* and he thought it as well expressed as the nature of language would admit. [Italics added.]

In this and other exchanges, the House debate made two things clear about the Bill of Rights and its religion clauses: (1) Madison was introducing the amendments not because he thought they were needed but because others did, and because he had promised to act according to their wishes; (2) the aim was to prevent Congress from establishing a "national" religion that would threaten the religious diversity of the states. Given the varied practices we have noted, ranging from establishments and doctrinal requirements for public office to relative toleration, any "national" religion would have been a source of angry discord.

Against that backdrop, the meaning of the establishment clause as it came out of conference should be crystal clear: "Congress shall make no law respecting an establishment of religion." The agency prohibited from acting is the national legislature; what it is prevented from doing is passing any law "respecting" an establishment of religion. In other words, Congress was forbidden to legislate at all concerning church establishments—either for or against. It was prevented from setting up a national established church; equally to the point, *it was prevented from interfering with the established churches in the states.*

Shield Becomes Sword

Though this history is often blurred over or ignored, it is

no secret, and its general features are sometimes acknowledged by liberal spokesmen. It may be conceded, for example, that the First Amendment was intended to be a prohibition against the federal government. But that guarantee was supposedly broadened by the Fourteenth Amendment, which "applied" the Bill of Rights against the states. Thus what was once prohibited only to the federal government is now also prohibited to the states.

Here we meet the Orwellian concept of "applying" a protection *of* the states *as a weapon against them*—using the First Amendment to achieve the very thing it was intended to prevent. The legitimacy of this reversal has been convincingly challenged by such constitutional scholars as Raoul Berger, Lino Graglia, and James McClellan. But for present purposes, let us simply *assume* the First Amendment restrictions on Congress were "applied" against the states. What then? What did this prohibit?

One thing we know for sure is that it *did not prohibit officially sponsored prayer.* As we have seen, Congress itself engaged in officially sponsored, tax-supported prayer, complete with paid official chaplains, from the very outset—and continues to do so to this day. Indeed, in one of the greatest ironies of this historical record, we see the practice closely linked with passage of the First Amendment—supplying a refutation of the Court's position that is as definitive as could be wished.

The language that had been debated off and on throughout the summer and then hammered out in conference finally passed the House of Representatives on September 24, 1789. *On the very next day,* the self-same House of Representatives passed a resolution calling for *a day of national prayer and thanksgiving.* Here is the language the House adopted: "We acknowledge with grateful hearts the many single favors of Almighty God, especially by affording them an opportunity peacefully to establish a constitutional government for their safety and happiness."

The House accordingly called on President Washington to issue a proclamation designating a national day of prayer and thanksgiving (the origin of our current legal holiday to this effect). This was Washington's response:

It is the duty of all nations to acknowledge the providence of Almighty God, to obey His will, to be grateful for His benefits, and humbly to implore His protection and favor.... That great and glorious Being who is the beneficent author of all the good that was, that is, or that ever will be, that we may then unite in rendering unto Him our sincere and humble thanks for His kind care and protection of the people.

Such were the official sentiments of Congress and the president immediately after the adoption of the First Amendment. These statements are far more doctrinal and emphatic than the modest prayer schoolchildren are forbidden to recite because it allegedly violates the First Amendment. If we accept the reasoning of the modern Court, as Robert Cord observes, *both Congress and George Washington violated the intended meaning of the First Amendment from its inception.*

The more logical conclusion, of course, is that Congress knew much better what it meant by the language adopted the preceding day than does our self-consciously evolving Court two centuries later. And, in the view of Congress, there was nothing either in law or in logic to bar it from engaging in officially sponsored, tax-supported prayer, then or ever. It follows that the amendment can't possibly bar the states from doing likewise.

Madison and Jefferson

To all of this, the liberal answer is, essentially: James Madison. Whatever the legislative history, we are informed, Madison in his subsequent writings took doctrinaire positions on church-state separation, and these should be read into the First Amendment. This, however, gets the matter topsy-turvy. Clearly, if the Congress that passed the First Amendment, and the states that ratified it, didn't agree with Madison's more stringent private notions, as they surely didn't, then these were not enacted. It is the common understanding of the relevant parties, not the ideas of a single individual, especially those expressed in other settings, that defines the purpose of a law or constitutional proviso.

Furthermore, the Court's obsession with the individual

views of Madison is highly suspect. It contrasts strangely with judicial treatment of his disclaimers in the House debate, and of his opinions on other constitutional matters. Madison held strict-constructionist views on the extent of federal power, arguing that the Constitution reserved undelegated authority to the states. *These* views of Madison are dismissed entirely by the Court. Thus we get a curious inversion: Madison becomes the Court's authority on the First Amendment, even though the notions he later voiced about this subject were not endorsed by others involved in its adoption. On the other hand, he isn't cited on the residual powers of the states, even though his statements on this topic were fully endorsed by other supporters of the Constitution and relied on by the poeple who voted its approval. It is hard to find a thread of consistency in this— beyond the obvious one of serving liberal ideology.

As peculiar as the Court's selective use of Madison is its resort to Jefferson. The anomaly here is that Jefferson was not a member of the Constitutional Convention, or of the Congress that considered the Bill of Rights, or of the Virginia ratifying convention. But he had strongly separationist views (up to a point) and had worked with Madison for disestablishment and religious freedom in Virginia. For the Court, this proves the First Amendment embodied Jefferson's statement in 1802, in a letter to the Baptists of Connecticut, about a "wall of separation."

Again we pass over the Lewis Carroll logic—in this case deducing the intent of an amendment adopted in 1789 from a letter written 13 years later by a person who had no official role in its adoption. Rather than dwelling on this oddity, we shall simply go to the record and see what Jefferson actually said about the First Amendment and its religion clauses. In his second inaugural address, for example, he said:

> In matters of religion, I have considered that its free exercise is placed by the Constitution independent of the powers of the general government. I have therefore undertaken on no occasion to prescribe the religious exercises suited to it. But I have left them as the Constitution found them, under the direction or discipline of state or church authorities acknowledged by the several religious societies.

Jefferson made the same point a few years later to a Presbyterian clergyman, who inquired about his attitude toward Thanksgiving proclamations:

> I consider the government of the United States as interdicted from intermeddling with religious institutions, their doctrines, discipline, or exercises. This results from the provision that no law shall be made respecting the establishment of religion or the free exercise thereof, but also from that which reserves to the states the powers not delegated to the United States. Certainly no power over religious discipline has been delegated to the general government. It must thus rest with the states as far as it can be in any human authority.

The irresistible conclusion is that there was no wall of separation between religious affirmation and civil government in the several states, nor could the First Amendment, with or without the Fourteenth Amendment, have been intended to create one. The wall of separation, instead, was *between the federal government and the states,* and was meant to make sure the central authority didn't meddle with the customs of local jurisdictions.

As a matter of constitutional law, the Court's position in these religion cases is an intellectual shambles—results-oriented jurisprudence at its most flagrant. An even greater scandal is the extent to which the Justices have rewritten the official record to support a preconceived conclusion: a performance worthy of regimes in which history is tailored to the interests of the ruling powers. In point of fact, America's constitutional settlement—up to and including the First Amendment—was the work of people who believed in God, and who expressed their faith as a matter of course in public prayer and other governmental practice.

A New Vision of Man: How Christianity Has Changed the Political Economy

Michael Novak

Michael Novak, former U.S. ambassador to the Human Rights Commission of the United Nations, currently holds the George Frederick Jewett Chair in Religion and Public Policy at the American Enterprise Institute in Washington, D.C.

He is the author of a dozen books, including: *The Catholic Ethic and the Spirit of Capitalism, This Hemisphere of Liberty, Freedom with Justice, The Spirit of Democratic Capitalism,* and *Belief and Unbelief.*

The Polish Solidarity movement and the Czech underground studied translations (often secretly and illegally) in the 1970s, as did members of pro-democratic movements in South Korea, Chile, Argentina, Venezuela, the Philippines, and China in the 1980s. Pope John Paul II's *Centesimus Annus,* published in 1991, is widely regarded as having been influenced by Mr. Novak's writings, and in her memoirs former British Prime Minister Margaret Thatcher noted that they "proved the intellectual basis of my approach to those great questions brought together in political parlance as 'the quality of life.'"

In May of 1994, Mr. Novak was awarded the Templeton Prize for Progress in Religion.

For centuries, scholars and laymen have studied the Bible's impact on our religion, politics, education, and culture, but very little serious attention has been devoted to its impact on our economics. It is as if our actions in the marketplace have nothing to do with our spiritual beliefs. Nothing could be further from the truth. My aim here is to demonstrate how Judeo-Christianity, and Jesus, in particular, revolutionized the political economy of the ancient world and how that revolution still profoundly affects the world today.

I wish to propose for your consideration the following

61

thesis: At least seven contributions made by Christian thinkers, meditating on the words and deeds of Jesus Christ, altered the vision of the good society proposed by the classical writers of Greece and Rome and made certain modern conceptions of political economy possible. Be warned that we are talking about foundational issues. The going won't be entirely easy.

Be warned, also, that I want to approach this subject in a way satisfying to secular thinkers. You shouldn't have to be a believer in Jesus in order to grasp the plausibility of my argument. In that spirit, let me begin, first, by citing Richard Rorty, who once wrote that as a progressive philosopher he owes more to Jesus for certain key progressive notions, such as compassion and equality, than to any of the classical writers. Analogously, in his book, *Why I am Not a Christian,* Bertrand Russell conceded that, although he took Jesus to be no more than a humanistic moral prophet, modern progressivism is indebted to Christ for the ideal of compassion.

In short, in order to recognize the crucial contributions that the coming of Christ brought into modern movements of political economy, one does not have to be a Christian. One may take a quite secular point of view and still give credit where credit is due.

Here, then, are the seven major contributions made by Jesus to our modern conceptions of political economy.

To Bring Judaism to the Gentiles

From Jerusalem, that crossroads between three continents open to the East and West, North and South, Jesus brought recognition of the One God, the Creator. The name this God gave to Himself is "I AM WHO AM"—He *is,* as opposed to the rest of us, who have no necessary or permanent hold on being. He is the One who IS; other things are those who are, but also are not. *He* is the Creator of all things. All things that are depend upon Him. As all things spring from His action in creating them, so they depend upon Him for their being maintained in existence, their "standing out from" nothingness [*Ex + sistere,* L., to stand out from].

The term "Creator" implies a free person; it suggests that

creation was a free act, an act that did not flow from necessity. It was an act of intelligence, it was a choice, and it was willed. The Creator knew what He was doing, and He willed it; that is, "He saw that it is good." From this notion of the One God/ Creator, three practical corollaries for human action follow.

Be intelligent. Made in the image of God, we should be attentive and intelligent, as our Creator is.

Trust liberty. As God loved us, so it is fitting for us to respond with love. Since in creating us He knew what He was doing and He willed it, we have every reason to trust His will. He created us with understanding and free will; creation was a free act. Since He made us in His image, well ought we to say with Jefferson: "The God who gave us life gave us liberty."

Understand that history has a beginning and an end. At a certain moment, time was created by God. Time is directed toward "building up the Kingdom of God ... on earth as in heaven." Creation is directed toward final union with its Creator.

As many scholars have noted, the idea of "progress" and the idea of "creation," are not Greek ideas—nor are they Roman. The Greeks preferred notions of the necessary procession of the world from a First Principle. While in a limited sense they understood the progress of ideas, skills, and technologies and also saw how these could be lost, in general, they viewed history as a cycle of endless return. They lacked a notion of historical progress. The idea of history as a category distinct from nature is a Hebrew rather than a Greek idea.

Analogously, as Lord Acton argued in the essays he prepared for his *History of Liberty,* liberty is an idea coincident with the spread of Christianity. Up to a point, the idea of liberty is a Jewish idea. Every story in the Bible is about a drama involving the human will. In one chapter, King David is faithful to his Lord; in another unfaithful. The suspense always lies in what he will choose next. Nonetheless, Judaism is not a missionary religion; normally one receives Judaism by being born of a Jewish mother; in this sense, Judaism is rooted in genealogy rather than in liberty. Beyond this point, Christianity expanded the notion of liberty and made it universal. The Christian idea of liberty remains rooted in the liberty of the Creator, as in Judaism. Through Christianity, this Jewish idea becomes the inheritance of all the other peoples on earth.

Recognition of the One God/Creator means that the fundamental attitude of human beings toward God is, and ought to be, receptivity. All that we are we have received from God. This is true both of our creation and our redemption. God acts first. We respond. Everything is a gift. "Everything we look upon is blessed" (Yeats). "Grace is everywhere" (Bernanos). Thus, offering thanksgiving is our first moral obligation.

It is difficult to draw out, in brief compass, all the implications for political economy of the fact that history begins in the free act of the Creator, who made humans in His image and who gave them both existence and an impulse toward communion with their first breath. In this act of creation, in any case, Jefferson properly located (and it was the sense of the American people) not only the origin of the inner core of human rights: ". . . and endowed by their Creator with certain inalienable rights, including . . . ," but also the perspective of providential history: "When in the course of human events . . ." The Americans were aware of creating something "new": a new world, a new order, a new science of politics. As children of the Creator, they felt no taboo against originality; on the contrary, they thought it their vocation.

Father, Son, and Holy Spirit

When Jesus spoke of God, He spoke of the communion of three persons in one. This means that, in God, the *mystery of being* and the *mystery of communion* are one. Unlike the Greeks such as Parmedides, Plato, and Aristotle, who thought of God or the *Nous* as One, living in solitary isolation, the Christian world was taught by Jesus to think of God as a communion of three. In other words, the mystery of communion, or community, is one with the very mystery of being. The sheer fact that we are alive sometimes comes over us at dusk on an autumn day, as we walk across a corn field and in the tang of the evening air hear a crow lift off against the sky. We may pause then to wonder, in admiration and gratitude. We could so easily have not been, and yet we are, at least for these fragile moments. Soon another generation will take our place, and tramp over the same field. We experience wonder at the sheer fact: At this moment, we *are*. And we also apprehend the fact that we are part of a long procession of the human community in time; and that we are, by the grace of God, one with God. To exist is already something to marvel at; so great a communion is even more so. Our wonder is not so much doubled; it is squared, infinitely multiplied.

This recognition of the Trinity is not without significance for political economy. First, it inspires us with a new respect for an ideal of community not often found on this earth, a community in which each person is separate, distinct, and independent, and yet in which there is, nonetheless, communion. It teaches us that the relation between community and person is deeper and richer that we might have imagined. Christians should not simply lose themselves in community, having their personality and independence merge into an undifferentiated mass movement. On the contrary, Christianity teaches us that in true community the distinctness and independence of each person are also crucial. Persons reach their full development only in community with others. No matter how highly developed in himself or herself, a totally isolated person, cut-off from others, is regarded as something of a monster. In parallel, a community that refuses to recognize the autonomy of individual persons often uses individuals as means to "the common good," rather than treating persons as ends in themselves. Such communities are coercive and tyrannical.

Christianity, in short, opens up the ideal of catholicity which has always been a mark of true Christianity. *Katholike* means all of humanity, the whole human world. In this world, persons, and even cultures, are distinct, and have their own autonomy and claim on our respect. *E pluribus unum.* The many form one; but the one does not melt the many into the lowest common denominator. The many retain their individual vitality, and for this they show gratitude to the community that allows them, in fact encourages them, to do so. Person and community must be defined in terms of each other.

The Children of God

In Plato's *Republic,* citizens were divided in this way: A few were of gold, a slightly larger body of silver, and the vast majority of lead. The last had the souls of slaves and, therefore, were properly enslaved. Only persons of gold are truly to be treated as ends in themselves. For Judaism and Christianity, on the contrary, the God who made every single child gave worth and dignity to each of them, however weak or vulnerable. "What you do unto the least of these, you do unto me." God identified Himself with the most humble and most vulnerable.

Our Creator knows each of us by name, and understands our own individuality with a far greater clarity that we ourselves do; after all, He made us. (Thomas Aquinas once wrote that God is infinite, and so when He creates human beings in His image, He must in fact create an infinite number of them to mirror back His own infinity.) Each of us reflects only a small fragment of God's identity. If one of us is lost, the image of God intended to be reflected by that one is lost. The image of God reflected in the human becomes distorted.

In this respect, Judaism and Christianity grant a fundamental equality in the sight of God to all human beings, whatever their talents or station. This equality arises because God penetrates *below* any artificial rank, honor, or station that may on the surface differentiate one from another. He sees past those things. He sees *into* us. He sees us as we are in our uniqueness, and it is that uniqueness that He values. Let us call this form of equality by the clumsy but useful name, *equality-as-uniqueness.* Before God, we have equal weight in our *uniqueness,* not because we are *the same,* but because each of us is *different.* Each is made by God after an original design.

This conception of equality-uniqueness is quite different from the modern "progressive" or socialist conception of *equality-sameness.* The Christian notion is not a levelling notion. Neither does it delight in uniformity. On the contrary, it tries to pay heed to, and give respect to, the unique image of God in each person.

For most of its history, Christianity, like Judaism, flourished in hierarchical societies. While recognizing that every single person lives and moves in sight of God's judgment and is equally a creature of God, Christianity has also rejoiced in the differences among us and between us. God did not make us equal in talent, ability, character, office, calling, or fortune.

Equality-uniqueness is not the same as equality-sameness. The first recognizes our claim to a unique identity and dignity. The second desires to take away what is unique and to submerge it in uniformity. Thus, modern movements such as socialism have taken the original Christian impulse of equality, which they inherited, and disfigured it. Like Christianity, modern socialist movements reject the stratification of citizens into gold, silver, and lead, as in Plato's scheme. But, since they are materialistic at root, their traditional impulse has been to pull people down, to place all on the same level, to enforce uniformity. This program is inexorably coercive, unlovely, and depressing.

Compassion

It is true that virtually all peoples have traditions of compassion for the suffering, care for those in need, and concern for others. However, in most religious traditions, these movements of the heart are limited to one's own family, kin, nation, or culture. In some cultures, young males in particular have to be hard and insensitive to pain, so that they will be sufficiently cruel to enemies. Terror is the instrument intended to drive outsiders away from the territory of the tribe. In principle (though not always in practice), Christianity opposes this limitation on compassion. It teaches people the impulse to reach out, especially to the most vulnerable, to the poor, the hungry, the wretched, those in prison, the hopeless, the sick, and others. It tells humans to love their enemies. It teaches a universal compassion. It teaches people to see the dignity even of those who in the eyes of the world have lost their dignity, and those who are helpless to act on their own behalf. This is the "solidarity" whose necessity for modernity Rorty perceives.

In the name of compassion, Christianity tries to humble the mighty and to prod the rich into concern for the poor. It does not turn the young male away from being a warrior, but it does teach him to model himself on Christ, and thus to become a new type of male in human history: the knight bound by a code of compassion, the gentleman. It teaches him to learn, to be meek, humble, peaceable, kind, and generous. It introduces a new and fruitful tension between the warrior and the gentlemen, magnanimity and humility, meekness and fierce ambition.

A Universal Family

Christianity has taught human beings that an underlying imperative of history is to bring about a law-like, peaceable community, among all people of good will on the entire earth. For political economy, Christianity proposes a new ideal: the entire human race is a universal family, created by the one same God, and urged to love that God. Yet at the same time, Christianity (like Judaism before it) is also the religion of a particular kind of God: not the Deity who looks down on all things from an olympian height but, in Christianity's case, a God who became *incarnate*. The Christian God, incarnate, was carried in the womb of a single woman, among a particular people, at a precise intersection of time and space, and nourished in a local community then practically unknown to the rest of the peoples on this planet. Christianity is a religion of the concrete and the universal. It pays attention to the flesh, the particular, the concrete, and each single intersection of space and time; its God is the God who made and cares for every lily of the field, every blade of grass, every hair on the head of each of us. Its God is the God of singulars, the God who Himself became a singular man. At the same time, the Christian God is the Creator of all.

In a sense, this Christian God goes beyond contemporary conceptions of "individualism" and "communitarianism." With 18th-century British statesman and philosopher Edmund Burke, Christianity sees the need for proper attention to every "little platoon" of society, to the immediate neighborhood, to the immediate family. Our social policies must be incarnate, must be rooted in the actual flesh of concrete people in their actual local, intimate worlds. At the same time, Christianity directs the attention of these little communities toward the larger communities of which they are a part. On the one hand, Christianity forbids them to be merely parochial or xenophobic. On the other hand, it warns them against becoming premature universalists, one-worlders, gnostics pretending to be pure spirits, and detached from all the limits and beauties of concrete flesh. Christianity gives warning against both extremes. It instructs us about the precarious balance between concrete and universal in our own nature. This is the mystery of catholicity.

"I Am the Truth"

The Creator of all things has total insight into all things. He knows what He has created. This gives the weak, modest minds of human beings the vocation to use their minds relentlessly, in order to penetrate the hidden layers of intelligibility that God has written into His creation. Everything in creation is in principle understandable: In fact, at every moment everything is understood by Him, who is eternal and therefore simultaneously present to all things. (In God there is no history, no past-present-future. In His insight into reality, all things are as if simultaneous. Even though in history they may unfold sequentially, they are all at once, that is, simultaneously, open to His contemplation.)

Our second president, John Adams, wrote that in giving us a notion of God as the Source of all truth, and the Judge of all, the Hebrews laid before the human race the possibility of civilization. Before the undeceivable Judgment of God, the Light of Truth cannot be deflected by riches, wealth, or worldly power. Armed with this conviction, Jews and Christians are empowered to use their intellects and to search without fear into the causes of things, their relationships, their powers, and their purposes. This understanding of Truth makes humans free. For Christianity does not teach that Truth is an illusion based upon the opinions of those in power, or merely a rationalization of powerful interests in this world. Christianity is not deconstructionist, and it is certainly not totalitarian. Its commitment to Truth beyond human purposes is, in fact, a rebuke to all totalitarian schemes and all nihilist cynicism.

Moreover, by locating Truth (with a capital T) in God, beyond our poor powers fully to comprehend, Christianity empowers human reason. It does so by inviting us to use our heads as best we can, to discern the evidences that bring us as close to Truth as human beings can attain. It endows human beings with a vocation to inquire endlessly, relentlessly, to give play to the unquenchable eros of the desire to understand—that most profoundly restless drive to know that teaches human beings their own finitude while it also informs them of their participation in the infinite.

The notion of Truth is crucial to civilization. As Thomas Aquinas held, civilization is constituted by conversation. Civilized persons persuade one another through argument. Barbarians club one another into submission. Civilization requires citizens to recognize that they do not possess the truth, but must be possessed by it, to the degree possible to them. Truth matters greatly. But Truth is greater than any one of us. We do not possess it; it possesses us. Therefore, humans must learn such civilizing habits as being respectful and open to others, listening attentively, trying to see aspects of the Truth that they do not as yet see. Because the search for Truth is vital to each of us, humans must argue with each other, urge each other onward, point out deficiencies in one another's arguments, and open the way for greater participation in the Truth by every one of us.

In this respect, the search for Truth makes us not only humble but also civil. It teaches us *why* we hold that every single person has an inviolable dignity: Each is made in the image of the Creator to perform noble acts, such as to understand, to deliberate, to choose, to love. These noble activities of human beings cannot be repressed without repressing the Image of God in them. Such an act would be doubly sinful. It violates the other person, and it is an offense against God.

One of the ironies of our present age is that the great philosophical advocates of the Enlightenment no longer believe in Reason (with a capital R). They have surrendered their confidence in the vocation of Reason to cynics such as to the post-modernists and deconstructionists. Such philosophers (*Sophists,* Socrates called them) hold that there is no Truth, that all things are relative, and that the great realities of life are power and interest. So we have come to an ironic pass. The children of the Enlightenment have abandoned Reason, while those they have considered unenlightened and living in darkness, the people of Jewish and Christian faith, remain today reason's (without a capital R) best defenders. For believing Jews and Christians ground their confidence in reason in the Creator of all reason, and their confidence in understanding in the One who understands everything He made—and loves it, besides.

There can be no civilization of reason, or of love, without this faith in the vocation of reason.

The Name of God: Mercy

Christianity teaches realistically not only the glories of human beings—their being made in the image of God—but also their sins, weaknesses, and evil tendencies. Judaism and Christianity are not utopian; they are quite realistic about human beings. They try to understand humans as they are, as God sees them both in their sins and in the graces that He grants them. This sharp awareness of human sinfulness was very important to the American founding.

Without ever using the term "original sin," the Founders were, in such documents as *The Federalist,* eloquent about the flaws, weaknesses, and evils to which human beings are prone. Therefore, they designed a republic that would last, not only among saints, but also among sinners. (There is no point in building a Republic for saints; there are too few of them; besides, the ones who do exist are too difficult to live with.) If you want to make a Republic that will last, you must construct it for sinners, because sinners are not just a moral majority, they are virtually a moral unanimity.

Christianity teaches that at every moment the God who made us is judging how well we make use of our liberty. And the first word of Christianity in this respect is: "Fear not. Be not afraid." For Christianity teaches that Truth is ordered to mercy. Truth is not, thank God, ordered first of all to justice. For if Truth were ordered to strict justice, not one of us would stand against the gale.

God is just, true, but the more accurate name for Him is not justice, but rather mercy. (The Latin root of this word conveys the idea more clearly: *Misericordia* comes from *miseris + cor*—give one's heart to *les miserables,* the wretched ones.) This name of God, *Misericordia,* according to St. Thomas Aquinas, is God's most fitting name. Toward our misery, He opens His heart. Precisely as sinners, He accepts us. "At the heart of Christianity lies the sinner," Charles Péguy wrote.

Yet mercy is only possible because of Judgment. Judgment Day is the Truth on which civilization is grounded. No matter what the currents of opinion in our time, or any time, may be; no matter what the powers and principalities may say or do; no matter what solicitations are pressing upon us from our families, friends, associates, and larger culture; no matter what the pressures may be—we will still be under the Judgment of the One who is undeceivable, who knows what is in us, and who knows the movements of our souls more clearly than we know them ourselves. In His Light, we are called to bring a certain honesty into our own lives, into our dealings with others, and into our respect for the Light that God has imparted to every human being. It is on this basis that human beings may be said to have inalienable rights, and dignity, and infinite worth.

Jesus, the Teacher

These seven recognitions lie at the root of Jewish-Christian civilization, the one that is today evasively called "Western civilization." From them, we get our deepest and most powerful notions of truth, liberty, community, person, conscience, equality, compassion, mercy, and virtue. These are the deepest ideals and energies working in our culture, as yeast works in dough, as a seed falling into the ground dies and becomes a spreading mustard tree.

These are practical recognitions. They have effects in

every person and in every moment of life, and throughout society. If you stifle these notions, if you wipe them out, the institutions of the free society become unworkable. In this sense, a U.S. Supreme Court Justice once wrote, "Our institutions presuppose a Supreme Being." They do not presuppose *any* Supreme Being. They presuppose the God of Judaism and Christianity. And not only our institutions presuppose these realities. So do our conceptions of our own identity, and the daily actions of our own lives. Remove these religious foundations from our intellects, our lives, and the free society—in its complex checks and balances, and its highly articulated divisions of power—becomes incoherent to understanding and unworkable in practice.

For the present form of the free society, therefore, we owe a great deal to the intervention of Jesus Christ in history. In bringing those of us who are not Jewish the Word that brings life, in giving us a nobler conception of what it is to be human, and in giving us insight into our own weaknesses and sins, Jesus shed light available from no other source. Better than the philosophers, Jesus Christ is the teacher of many lessons indispensible for the working of the free society. These lessons may be, and have been secularized—but not without losing their center, their coherence, and their long-term persuasive power.

But that alone would be as nothing, of course, if we did not learn from Jesus that we, all of us, participate in His life, and in living with Him, live in, with and through the Father and the Holy Spirit in a glorious community of love. For what would it profit us, if we gained the whole world, and all the free institutions that flourish with it, and lost our own souls?

Introducing the Orthodox Church

Peter E. Gillquist

The Very Reverend Father Peter E. Gillquist began his career in the 1960s as a regional director for Campus Crusade for Christ and later as director of development for the University of Memphis. In the early 1970s, he turned to freelance writing and editing. This led to his appointment as senior editor with Thomas Nelson Publishers in 1975, a post he held until 1986. He became president of the Evangelical Orthodox Church (EOC), based in Santa Barbara, in 1977.

In 1987 the EOC was received into canonical Orthodoxy and Father Gillquist became archpriest and chairman of the department of missions and evangelism in the Antiochian Orthodox Christian Archdiocese of North America. He is also director of the Conciliar Press and publisher of *Again* magazine. He is the author of numerous books, including *Love Is Now, Becoming Orthodox: A Journey to the Ancient Christian Faith,* and *Metropolitan Philip, His Life and Dreams.*

No discussion of faith in the modern age would be complete without addressing the historical roots of Christianity. After all, we must learn where we have been in order to know where we are and where we are going. Addressing the historical roots of Christianity requires us to hearken back to the founding of the Orthodox Church.

Exactly what is the Orthodox Church? Many people have heard of the Russian Orthodox Church, which celebrated its one thousandth birthday in 1988, or the Greek Orthodox Church, which was born centuries earlier. But what about Orthodoxy itself—what is it, and what are its origins?

The Church in the New Testament

To answer the question, we must turn to the pages of the New Testament, specifically to the Book of Acts and the birth of the Church at Pentecost. On that day the Holy Spirit descended on the Twelve Apostles and those gathered in the Upper Room, and by afternoon some three thousand souls believed in Christ and were baptized. The Scriptures record that when the first Christian community began, "they continued steadfastly in the apostles' doctrine and fellowship, in the breaking of bread, and in prayers" (Acts 2:42).

From Jerusalem, faith in Christ spread throughout Judea, to Samaria (Acts 8:5–39), to Antioch and to the Gentiles (Acts 11:19–26). Soon there were new converts and new churches throughout Asia Minor and the Roman Empire as recorded in Acts and the Epistles.

The Church, of course, was not simply another organization in Roman society. The Lord Jesus Christ had given the promise of the Holy Spirit to "guide you into all truth" (John 16:13). With the fulfillment of that promise beginning with Pentecost, the Church bore more than mere institutional status. She is not an organization with mystery but a mystery with organization. St. Paul called the Church "a dwelling place of God in the Spirit" (Eph. 2:22). The Church is a dynamic organism, the living body of Jesus Christ. She makes an indelible impact in the world, and those who live in her life and share her faith are personally transformed.

But the New Testament also reveals that the historic Church had her share of problems. All was not perfection. Some individuals within the Church even sought to lead her off the path the Apostles established, and they had to be suffered with along with the errors they invented. Even whole local communities lapsed on occasion and were called to repentance. The church in Laodicea is a vivid example (Rev. 3:14–22). Discipline was administered for the sake of purity in the Church. But there was growth and maturation, even as the Church was attacked from within and without. The same Spirit who gave her birth gave her power for purity and correction, and she stood strong and grew, eventually invading the whole of the Roman Empire.

The Early Centuries

As the Church moves from the pages of the New Testament and on into the succeeding centuries of her history, her growth and development can be traced in terms of specific categories. The first is a category important for all Christian people: *doctrine.* Did she maintain the truth of God as given by Christ and His Apostles? Second, what about *worship?* Is there a discernible way in which the people of God have offered a sacrifice of praise and thanksgiving to Him? Third, consider Church *government.* What sort of polity did the Church practice?

1. *Doctrine:* Not only did the Church begin under the teaching of the Apostles, but she was also instructed to "stand fast and hold the traditions which you were taught, whether by word or our epistle" (2 Thess. 2:15). The Apostle Paul insisted that those matters delivered by him and his fellow Apostles, both in person and in the writings that would come to be called the New Testament, be adhered to carefully. Thus followed such appropriate warnings as "in the name of our Lord Jesus Christ...withdraw from every brother who walks disorderly and not according to the tradition which he received from us" (2 Thess. 3:6). The doctrines taught by Christ and His Disciples are to be safeguarded by "the church of the living God, the pillar and ground of the truth" (1 Tim. 3:15) and are not open for negotiation. The Church was still young when a way had to be found for providing this safeguard.

Midway through the first century, a dispute arose in Antioch over adherence to Old Testament laws. The matter could not be settled there; outside help was needed. The leaders of the Antiochian Church, the community which had earlier dispatched Paul and Barnabas as missionaries, brought the matter to Jerusalem for consideration by the Apostles and elders there. The matter was discussed, and debated, and a written decision was forthcoming.

James, the brother of the Lord and the first bishop of Jerusalem, put forth the solution to the problem. This settlement, agreed to by all concerned at what is known as the Council of Jerusalem (Acts 15:1–35), set the pattern for the use of church councils in the centuries ahead to settle doctrinal and moral issues that arose. Thus, throughout the history of the Church, we find scores of such councils on various levels to settle matters of dispute and to deal with those who do not adhere to the apostolic faith.

The first three hundred years of Christian history were also marked by the appearance of certain heresies or false teachings such as secret philosophic schemes for the elite (Gnosticism), dazzling prophetic aberrations (Montanism), and grave errors regarding the three Persons of the Trinity (Sabellianism).

Then, in the early fourth century, a heresy with potential for Church-wide disruption appeared, propagated by one Arius, a presbyter in Alexandria, Egypt. He denied the eternality of the Son of God, claiming, contrary to the Apostles' doctrine, that the Son was a created being who came into existence at a point in time, and thus was not truly God. This deadly error struck the Church like a cancer. Turmoil spread almost everywhere. The first Church-wide gathering, the first Ecumenical Council, met in Nicea in A.D. 325 to address this issue. Some three hundred bishops, along with many priests, deacons, and laymen, rejected the new teaching of Arius and his associates, upholding the Apostles' doctrine of Christ, affirming the eternality of the Son and His consubstantiality with the Father. Their proclamation of the apostolic teaching concerning Christ included a creed, which, with the additions concerning the Holy Spirit made in 381 A.D. at the Council of Constantinople, forms the document today called the Nicene Creed.

Between the years 325 A.D. and 787 A.D., seven such Church-wide conclaves were held, meeting in the cities of Nicea, Ephesus, Chalcedon, and Constantinople. Known as the seven Ecumenical Councils, all dealt first and foremost with some specific challenge to the apostolic teaching about Jesus Christ. The Third Ecumenical Council (431 A.D.), for instance, condemned the Nestorians—those who would divide

Christ into two persons, one human and the other divine. The Nestorians were concentrated in Persia and eastward, and when some of the Nestorian bishops would not accept the decision of the Council, the Church experienced the first territorial schism. Active evangelicals, the Nestorians formed communities in Arabia, India, and as far away as China. A remnant still carries on a precarious existence in Kurdistan, Iraq, Syria, and the United States.

Among the issues addressed by the Fourth Ecumenical Council (451 A.D) was the heresy of the Monophysites, who claimed that there is but one nature in Christ. Some claimed that the two natures in Christ were mingled into one making Him neither God nor man. Others believed that the divine nature had swallowed up the human nature, and still other Monophysites believed that the Son had left His divine nature behind when He became man. Again a segment of the church departed with the heretics. The Monophysite church still exists in Syria, Armenia, and Egypt. There is encouraging news, however, for the churches which left after the Council have recently worked out an agreement with the Orthodox Church, satisfying Orthodox theologians of their doctrinal correctness. Consequently, a break of 1,500 is on the verge of being healed.

For the first thousand years of Christian history, the entire Church, save for the heretics, embraced and defended the New Testament apostolic faith. There was no consequential division. This one faith, preserved through all trials, attacks and tests, this apostolic doctrine was called "the Orthodox faith."

2. *Worship:* Doctrinal purity was tenaciously maintained, but true Christianity is far more than adherence to a set of correct beliefs alone. The life of the Church is centrally expressed in her worship and adoration of God the Father, Son, and Holy Spirit. Jesus Himself told the woman at the well, "the hour is coming, and now is, when the true worshippers will worship the Father in spirit and truth; for the Father is seeking such to worship Him" (John 4:23).

At the Last Supper, Jesus instituted the Eucharist, the communion service, when He took bread and wine, gave a blessing, and said to His disciples, "This is My body which is given for you; do this in remembrance of Me," and "This cup is the new covenant in My blood, which is shed for you" (Luke 22:19, 21). The Church participated in communion at least each Lord's Day (Acts 20:7, 11). From such first- and second-century sources as the *Didache,* the letters of St. Ignatius of Antioch and the writings of St. Justin Martyr, we are assured the Eucharist is the very center of Christian worship from the apostolic era on.

Also, just as the Law, the Psalms, and the Prophets were read in the Temple worship and the synagogue in Israel, so the Church also immediately gave high priority to the public reading of Scripture and to preaching in her worship, along with the Eucharistic meal.

Even before the middle of the first century, Christian worship was known by the term *liturgy,* which literally means "the common works" or "the work of the people." The early liturgy of the Church's worship was composed of two essential parts: (1) the liturgy of the word, including hymns, Scripture reading, and preaching; and (2) the liturgy of the faithful, composed of intercessory prayers, the kiss of peace, and the Eucharist. From virtually the beginning, Christian worship has had a definable shape or form which continues to this day.

Modern Christians advocating freedom from liturgy in worship are sometimes surprised to learn that spontaneity was never the practice in the ancient Church! A basic pattern or shape of Christian worship was observed from the start, and, as the Church grew and matured, the liturgy matured as well. Hymns, Scripture readings, and prayers were a part of the basic foundation. A clear, purposeful procession through the year was forthcoming, which marked—and joined in word, song, and praise—the birth, ministry, death, resurrection, and ascension of the Lord Jesus Christ, and sanctified crucial aspects of Christian life and experience. The Christian life was lived in reality in the worship of the Church. Far from being just a boring routine, the ritual worship of the historic Church participated in the unfolding drama of the richness and mystery of the Gospel itself.

Further, specific landmarks in our salvation and walk with

Christ were celebrated and sanctified. Baptism and the anointing with oil, or "chrismation," were there from the start. Marriage, healing, confession of sin, and ordination to the ministry of the Gospel are other early rites in the Church. On each of these occasions Christians understood that in a great mystery, grace and power from God were being given according to the individual need of each person. The Church saw these events as holy moments in her life and called them mysteries or sacraments.

3. *Government:* No one seriously questions whether the Apostles of Christ led the Church at her beginning. They had been given the commission to preach the Gospel (Matt. 28:19, 20) and the authority to forgive or retain sins (John 20:23). Theirs was by no means a preaching-only mission. They built the Church under Christ's headship. To govern it, three definite and permanent offices, as taught in the New Testament, were in evidence.

a. *The office of bishop:* The apostles themselves were the first bishops in the Church. Even before Pentecost, after Judas had turned traitor, Peter declared in applying Psalm 109:8, "Let another take his office" (Acts 1:20). This refers, of course, to the office of bishop. Some have mistakenly argued the office of bishop was a later invention. Quite to the contrary, the Apostles were themselves bishops, and they appointed bishops to succeed them to oversee the Church in each locality.

Occasionally, the objection is still heard that the office of bishop and presbyter were originally identical. The terms are used interchangeably in the New Testament while the Apostles were present, with a bishop being the presiding elder in a local church. After the Apostles' deaths, however, the offices of bishop and presbyter became distinct throughout the Church. Ignatius of Antioch, consecrated bishop by A.D. 70 in the Church from which Paul and Barnabas had been sent out, writes just after the turn of the century that bishops appointed by the Apostles, surrounded by their presbyters, were everywhere in the Church.

b. *The office of presbyter:* Elders or presbyters are mentioned very early in the life of the Church in Acts and the Epistles. Evidently, in each place a Christian community developed, elders were appointed by the Apostles to pastor the people.

As time passed, presbyters were referred to in the short form of the word as "prests," then as "priests," in full view of the fact that the Old Covenant priesthood had been fulfilled in Christ and that the Church is corporately a priesthood of believers. The priest was not understood as an intermediary between God and the people nor as a dispenser of grace. The role of the priest was to be the presence of Christ in the Christian community, and in the very capacity of being the presence of the Chief Shepherd, Jesus Christ, the priest was to safeguard the flock of God.

c. *The office of deacon:* The third order or office in the government of the New Testament Church was the deacon. At first the Apostles fulfilled this office themselves, but with the rapid growth of the Church, seven initial deacons were selected (Acts 6:1–7) to help carry the responsibility of service to those in need. One of these deacons, Stephen, became the first martyr of the Church.

Through the centuries, the deacons have not only served the material needs of the Church but have held a key role in the liturgical life of the Church as well. Often called "the eyes and ears of the bishop," many deacons have become priests and ultimately entered the episcopal office.

In ancient times the authority of the bishop, presbyter, and deacon was not understood as being apart from the people but always from among the people. In turn, the people of God were called to submit to those who ruled over them (Heb. 13:17), and they were also called to give their agreement to the direction of the leaders for the Church. On a number of occasions in history, that "Amen" was not forthcoming, and the bishops of the Church took note and changed course. Later in history, many Church leaders departed from the ancient model and usurped authority for themselves. In the minds of some, this brought the ancient model into question, but the problem was not in the model. It was in the deviation.

Also, it was the ministry of the Apostles that brought the

people of God together as the laity. Far from being just a body of observers, the laity is vital in the effectiveness of the Church. Its members are the recipients and active users of the gifts and grace of the Spirit. Each member has a role in the life and function of the Church. Each is to supply something to the whole (1 Cor. 12:7). The responsibility of the bishops, the priests, and the deacons is to be sure that this is a reality for the laity.

The worship of the Church at the close of its first one thousand years had substantially the same shape from place to place. The doctrine was the same. The whole Church confessed one creed, the same in every place, and had weathered many attacks. The government of the Church was recognizably one everywhere, and this one Church was the Orthodox Church.

Disagreements Between West and East

Tensions began to mount as the first millennium was drawing to a close. While numerous doctrinal, political, economic, and cultural factors were working to separate the Church in an East-West division, two major issues ultimately emerged above others: (1) that one man, the Pope of Rome, considered himself the universal bishop of the Church; and (2) the addition of a novel clause to the Church's creed.

1. *The Papacy:* Among the Twelve, Saint Peter was early acknowledged as the leader of the Apostles. He was spokesman for the Twelve before and after Pentecost. He was the first bishop of Antioch and later bishop of Rome. No one challenged his role.

After the death of the Apostles, and as leadership in the Church developed, the bishop of Rome came to be recognized as first in honor, even though all bishops were equals. But after nearly three hundred years, the bishop of Rome slowly began to assume a role of superiority over the others, ultimately claiming to be the only true successor to Peter. The vast majority of the other bishops of the Church never questioned

Rome's primacy of honor, but they patently rejected the Roman bishop's claim as the universal head of the Church on earth. This assumption of papal power became one major factor in rending the Roman Church, and all those it could gather with it, from the historic Orthodox Church.

2. *The Addition to the Creed:* A disagreement concerning the Holy Spirit also began to develop in the Church. Does the Holy Spirit proceed from the Father? Or does He proceed from the Father and the Son?

Our Lord Jesus Christ teaches, "But when the Helper comes, whom I shall send to you from the Father, the Spirit of truth who *proceeds from the Father,* He will testify of Me" (John 15:26, emphasis mine). This is the basic statement in the New Testament about the Holy Spirit "proceeding," and it is clear: He "proceeds from the Father" Thus, when the ancient council at Constantinople (A.D. 381) reaffirmed the Creed of Nicea (A.D. 325), it expanded that Creed to proclaim these familiar words: "And in the Holy Spirit, the Lord and Life Giver, Who proceeds from the Father, Who is worshipped and glorified together with the Father and the Son...."

Two hundred years later, however, at a local council in Toledo, Spain (A.D. 589), King Reccared declared, "The Holy Spirit also should be confessed by us and taught to proceed from the Father and the Son." The king may have meant well, but he was contradicting Jesus's teaching, confessed by the entire Church, concerning the Holy Spirit. Unfortunately, the local Spanish council agreed with his error, and, centuries later, in what was at least partially a politically motivated move, the Pope of Rome unilaterally changed the universal creed of the Church *without* an ecumenical council. Though this change was initially rejected in both East and West even by some of Rome's closest neighboring bishops, the Pope eventually managed to get the West to capitulate. The consequence, of course, in the Western Church has been the tendency to relegate the Holy Spirit to a lesser place than God the Father and God the Son. The change may appear small, but the consequences have proven disastrous. This issue, with the Pope departing from the Orthodox doctrine of the Church, became another instrumental cause separating the Roman Church from the historic Orthodox Church, the New Testament Church.

The Great Schism

Conflict between the Roman Pope and the East mounted—especially in the Pope's dealings with the Bishop, or Patriarch, of Constantinople. The Pope even went so far as to claim the authority to decide who should be the bishop of Constantinople, in marked violation of historical precedent. No longer operating within the government of the New Testament Church, the Pope appeared to be seeking by political means to bring the whole Church under his domination.

Bizarre intrigues followed, one upon the other, as a series of Roman popes pursued this unswerving goal of attempting to control all Christendom. Perhaps the most incredible incident of these political, religious, and even military schemes occurred in the year 1054. A cardinal, sent by the Pope, slapped a document on the altar of the Church of Holy Wisdom in Constantinople during the Sunday worship, excommunicating the patriarch of Constantinople from the Church.

The Pope, of course, had no legitimate right to do this, but the repercussions were staggering. Some dismal chapters of Church history were written during the next decades. The ultimate consequence of the Pope's action was that the whole Roman Catholic Church ended up divided from the New Testament faith of Orthodox Christianity. The schism has never been healed.

As the centuries passed, conflict continued. Attempts at reunion failed, and the Roman Church drifted further from its historical roots.

Further Divisions in the West

During the centuries after A.D. 1054, the growing distinction between East and West was becoming indelibly marked in history. The Eastern Church maintained the full stream of

New Testament faith, worship, and practice—all the while enduring great persecution. The Western or Roman Church bogged down in many complex problems. Then, less than five centuries after Rome committed itself to its unilateral alteration of doctrine and practice, another upheaval occurred—this time inside the Western gates.

Although many in the West had spoken out against Roman domination and practice in earlier years, now a little-known German monk named Martin Luther inadvertently launched an attack against certain Roman Catholic practices which ended up affecting world history. His list of Ninety-Five Theses was nailed to the Church door at Wittenberg in 1517, signaling the start of what came to be called the Protestant Reformation. Luther had intended no break with Rome, but he could not be reconciled to its papal system of government as well as other doctrinal issues. He was excommunicated in 1521, and the door to future unity in the West slammed shut with a resounding crash.

The reforms Luther sought in Germany were soon accompanied by demands of Ulrich Zwingli in Zurich, John Calvin in Geneva, and hundreds of others all over Western Europe. Fueled by complex political, social, and economic factors in addition to the religious problems, the Reformation spread like a raging fire into virtually every nook and cranny of the Roman Church. The ecclesiastical monopoly to which it had grown accustomed was greatly diminished, and massive division replaced unity. The ripple effect of that division impacts us even today, as the Protestant movement continues to split.

If trouble on the European continent were not trouble enough, the Church of England was in the process of going its own way as well. Henry VIII, amidst his marital problems, replaced the Pope of Rome with himself as head of the Church of England. For only the few short years that Mary was on the throne did the Pope again have ascendancy in England. Elizabeth I returned England to Protestantism, and the English Church would soon experience even more division.

As decade followed decade in the West, the branches of Protestantism continued to divide. There were even branches that insisted they were neither Protestant nor Roman Catholic.

All seemed to share a mutual dislike for the Bishop of Rome and the practices of his Church, and most wanted far less centralized forms of leadership. While some, such as the Lutherans and Anglicans, held on to certain forms of liturgy and sacrament, others, such as the Reformed Churches and the even more radical Anabaptists and their descendants, questioned and rejected many biblical ideas of hierarchy, sacrament, and historic tradition, thinking they were freeing themselves only of Roman Catholicism. To this day, many sincere, modern, professing Christians will reject even the biblical data that speak of historic Christian practice, simply because they think such historic practices are "Roman Catholic." To use the old adage, they threw the baby out with the bath water without even being aware of it.

Thus, while retaining in varying degrees portions of foundational Christianity, neither Protestantism nor Catholicism can lay historic claim to being the true New Testament Church. In dividing from Orthodox Christianity, Rome forfeited its place in the Church of the New Testament. In the divisions of the Reformation, the Protestants—as well-meaning as they might have been—failed to return to the New Testament Church.

The Orthodox Church Today

That original Church, the Church of Peter, Paul, and the Apostles—despite persecution, political oppression, and desertion on certain of its flanks—miraculously carries on today the same faith and life of the Church of the New Testament. Admittedly, the style of Orthodoxy looks complicated to the modern Protestant eye, but given a historical understanding of how the Church has progressed, it may be seen that the simple Christ-centered faith of the Apostles is fully preserved in its doctrines, practices, services, and even in its architecture.

In Orthodoxy today, as in years gone by, the basics of Christian doctrine, worship, and government are never up for alteration. One cannot be an Orthodox priest, for example, and reject the divinity of Christ, His virgin birth, resurrection, ascension into heaven, and second coming. The Church simply has not left its course in nearly two thousand years. It is

One, Holy, Catholic, and Apostolic. It is the New Testament Church.

Orthodoxy is also, in the words of one of her bishops, "the best-kept secret in America." Although there are more than 225 million Orthodox Christians in the world today, many in the West are not familiar with the Church. In North America, for example, the Orthodox Church has, until recently, been largely restricted to ethnic communities, not spreading much beyond the parishes of the committed immigrants that in the past brought the Church to the shores of this continent.

Still, the Holy Spirit has continued His work, causing new people to discover this Church of the New Testament. People have begun to find Orthodox Christianity through the writings of the early Church Fathers and through the humble witness of contemporary Orthodox Christians. Significant numbers of evangelical, Episcopalians, and mainline Protestants are becoming Orthodox, and Orthodox student groups are springing up on campuses worldwide. The word is getting out.

Learning More About the Orthodox Church

What, then, is the Orthodox Church? It is the first Christian Church in history, the Church founded by the Lord Jesus Christ, described in the pages of the New Testament. Her history can be traced in unbroken continuity all the way back to Christ and His Twelve Apostles.

What is it that is missing in the non-Orthodox Churches—even the best of them? Fullness. For the fullness of the New Testament faith is to be found only in the New Testament Church. Being in the Church does not guarantee all those in it will take advantage of the fullness of the faith, but that fullness is there for those who do.

For persons who seriously desire the fullness of Orthodox Christianity, action must be taken. Being aware of this ancient Church is not enough. There must be a return to this Church of the New Testament. In our day many people have taken ample time to investigate and decide about the Roman Catholic faith, the Baptist faith, the Lutheran faith, and so on. But relatively few have taken a serious look at the Orthodox Church. Three specific suggestions will provide those interested with a tangible means of becoming acquainted with Orthodox Christianity on a personal basis.

1. *Visit:* Look up "Orthodox" or "Eastern Orthodox" in the "Churches" section of the yellow pages, or ask a neighbor the whereabouts of the nearest Orthodox parish. Pay a visit—several visits. Meet the priest, and ask him to help you study and learn. And be prepared to exercise patience—sometimes a portion of the liturgy is not in English! The Service Book in the pew will help.

2. *Read:* There are a number of books and periodicals immensely helpful to people seeking to learn about the Orthodox Church. They include *The Orthodox Church* by KALLISTOS (Timothy) Ware; *For the Life of the World* by Alexander Schmemann; *The Apostolic Fathers* edited by Jack N. Sparks; *Becoming Orthodox* by Peter E. Gillquist; *Divine Energy* by Jon E. Braun; and *Again* magazine published by the Concilar Press.

3. *Write:* The staff at Conciliar Press (P.O. Box 76, Ben Lomond, CA 95005–0076) has volunteered to answer questions regarding the Orthodox Church and to suggest further reading. Send your name and address with a request for information.

In a day when Christians are realizing anew the centrality and importance of worship, of the Church as the body of Christ, and the need to preserve true Christian faith, the doors of Orthodoxy are open wide. The invitation is extended to "come and see." Examine her faith, her worship, her history, her commitment to Christ, her love for God the Father, and her communion with the Holy Spirit.

For two thousand years the Orthodox Church has, by God's mercy, kept the faith delivered to the saints. Within her walls is the fullness of the salvation which was realized when "God so loved the world that He gave His only begotten Son, that whoever believes in Him should not perish but have everlasting life" (John 3:16).

The Great Jubilee

Clark H. Pinnock

Since 1977, Clark H. Pinnock has been Professor of Christian Interpretation at McMaster Divinity College in Ontario, where he teaches courses on systematic theology, theological method, social ethics, philosophy of religion, and other related subjects. He is also a member of the advanced degree faculty at the Toronto School of Theology. Formerly, he taught at Regent College, Trinity Evangelical Divinity School, New Orleans Baptist Theological Seminary, and the University of Manchester, UK. He earned his Ph.D. at Manchester in New Testament studies.

Dr. Pinnock's many books include: *Unbounded Love: Good News Theology for the 21st Century, The Openness of God* (with others), *A Wideness in God's Mercy, Four Views of Hell, Theological Crossfire: An Evangelical/Liberal Dialogue* (with Delwin Brown), *The Scripture Principle,* and *Reason Enough.*

When I learned of the theme of the conference, which is to reflect upon the divine-human encounter at the end of the millennium, I was reminded of the words of Pope John Paul II in his encyclical on the Holy Spirit (1986) where he speaks of a great jubilee that will mark the passage from the second to the third Christian millennium and where he instructs us to remember the gift of Jesus through the Spirit in that year. He writes: "The Church's mind and heart turn to the Holy Spirit as this twentieth century draws to a close and the third millennium since the coming of Jesus Christ into the world approaches, and as we look towards the great jubilee with which the Church will celebrate the event" (*Dominum et Vivificantem,* 69). I am suggesting that we heed his invitation to focus on the Holy Spirit in this lecture by taking up some of the pope's themes in the encyclical. I hope that you will find some of them timely and relevant.

When you read the encyclical, you discover that Pope John Paul has a comprehensive vision of the Holy Spirit, a vision which overcomes a neglect of certain aspects of the doctrine in the church's theology and life. One receives the impression of a profound pastor who not only operates on the cutting edge of theological conversation but who longs for the Spirit to move again in power in human history and experience. As we proceed, we might take note of his reference to mind *and* heart not just to the mind. He adds a reference to the heart because the Spirit is a mysterious power revealed mostly by symbols such as water and fire, not in abstract formulae. While the mind should be active in searching out the meaning of these signs, a knowledge of the Spirit does not come only by way of the intellect but arises in hearts which wait upon God in poverty of spirit. The heart and the mind thus complement one another in the investigation of this subject and it is important that our hearts be open to being drawn into the mystery of God's love.

How the Spirit Relates to the Being of God

Part one of the encyclical touches a most fundamental issue. How the Spirit relates to the being of God. In line with the creedal foundations of faith, it refers to the Spirit's participation in the everlasting, loving communion of the Trinity. The Apostle John states that God is love, and this love is revealed in the love which the Father and the Son have for each other and in the mutual giving and receiving of love between the Father, Son, and Spirit. Christians understand God to be a living, relational Being and see the Spirit participating in this communion and communication of persons. The Spirit is engaged in what John of Damascus calls a "dance," which is his picture of the mutual love and coherence of Father, Son, and Spirit—a fellowship into which, remarkably, we creatures are summoned to participate by the grace of God.

The Spirit is less defined as a person compared with Father and Son. One might say that they are given faces but the Spirit remains more mysterious and less focused. We are more familiar with familial images of father and son than we are with a mighty wind blowing where it wills. This reduced focus comes out when the third person is simply called "Spirit," which is the general term used for the Godhead (John 4:24). In spite of this, the Spirit seems always to be associated with the love of Father and Son, as witness to it and participant in it and thus is identified by theologians such as Augustine and Richard St. Victor as the link between the Father and Son in their love (*condilectus*).

An analogy is sometimes drawn from the context of marriage. As a husband and a wife fashion a community in the birth of a child, so the Father and the Son perfect the love between them by sharing it with a third person. Their own love is enriched by sharing it with the Spirit who also occupies the space of the relationship of Father and Son. We should see the Spirit as proceeding from their love in a mysterious way, making it a love which is open and not exclusive.

The Spirit does not call attention to itself but seems to play a modest and self-effacing role. It seems to want to be known, not in ways which would highlight its own personality, but as the power of love which facilitates the purposes of God. St. Paul's statement seems to be of central importance: "God's love has been poured out into our hearts through the Holy Spirit" (Rom 5:5). Though there must be much more that is true about its identity, the Spirit is revealed as the power of God's love which touches, quickens, and warms us. Tertullian uses this analogy: think of the Father as the orb of the sun, and Jesus as the beam of light emanating from it, and the Spirit as its warmth and energy (*Against Praxeas,* 8). The Spirit is the irradiation of God's love, which ravishes our hearts and enables them to love in return. The Spirit is the mystery of God's engagement with the world and his empowering presence from the beginning of time.

The relevance of this vision can be seen in relation to modern atheism. Atheism arose in part (I think) on account of an eclipse of this captivating vision of God as open, loving, and dynamic communion. More basic than the question, "Does God exist?" is the question, "What do you mean by God?" And in reply to that question, the encyclical directs us to a model of God who shines forth in self-giving love, sweeps away our fears, and summons us to seek union with God.

The Breath of Life

A second area of importance in the doctrine of the Spirit to which the encyclical points is its role in nature and in creation as "the breath of life which causes all creation, all history, to flow together to its ultimate end, in the infinite ocean of God" (95). God the Trinity, because it is overflowing love, chooses to create a world with creatures capable of loving God and of loving fellow creatures. Because God is love, he wants to make love and mutuality abound and sends forth the Spirit to implement this goal and bring this plans to fruition. The psalmist relates the Spirit and nature: "When you send forth your Spirit, they are created and you renew the face of the ground" (Psalm 104:30).

At a time when people are concerned about the natural history and historical future of the planet, it is expedient to link the Spirit and creation. Modern science recognizes that nature is not a machine but a dynamic and interrelated process. This gives theology the opportunity to see the Spirit as the ground of life in the world and the one who calls it forth. The Spirit is the power present from the first stirrings of earth's history, sustaining the world and moving its creatures to transcend themselves. The encyclical invites us to view the Spirit as God's immanent creative activity, alive in all that happens in nature, and forming the ecology in which creatures capable of love can arise and flourish. This move relating the Spirit and nature helps us with the doctrine of creation in an age of scientific cosmology.

Of particular value to my way of thinking is the alternative this possibility supplies to the unhappy dualism we often face between naturalistic evolution and theistic creation—between evolution understood as chance and necessity and creation understood as a set of forms which do not undergo transformation through time. By referring to the Spirit in nature, it is possible to combine creation and evolution by thinking of the

Spirit guiding the process that leads to life by calling into existence the many conditions which make it possible. From the exuberance of trinitarian love comes the desire for creatures capable of loving and from the Spirit comes the power and wisdom to make it happen. The Spirit stands behind the creative process which produces more than is expected and moves towards ever more complex forms and ultimately to human life. One of Job's friends was on target: "The Spirit of God has made us, and the breath of the Almighty has given us life" (Job 33:4). In the service of the creator, the Spirit supplies the inner-worldly direction and drive toward the goal of humanization, a trajectory which finds fulfillment in Jesus Christ.

I appreciate how the encyclical proposes to think of nature in relation to the Spirit, hovering over the universe like a mother bird hatching order from chaos. We do not need to conceptualize the creation event as a one-time action that produces a world and then ceases to operate. One may image a continual energizing of world by the Spirit throughout its long history (*creatio continua*). I find it helpful to be able to think of the Spirit as pervading the universe, knitting things together and holding the world open for divine love.

The Incarnation

The third contribution which strikes me is the way the encyclical speaks of the Spirit in relation to the Incarnation (69–77). Often the Incarnation is thought of apart from the Spirit as the Word made flesh, in order to become a sacrifice for the sins of the world, placed in a forensic setting. By bringing the Spirit into proximity with Christology, it invites us to think of the work of Christ along other lines. Specifically it lets us view Jesus in terms of the mission of the Spirit and conceptualize his work as a Spirit-empowered representative on behalf of human life which fulfills the purpose of creation and heals humanity through a recapitulation of our human journey. It invites us to recover the "soteriology" of Irenaeus and the early Greek fathers who taught in these terms. I applaud the way the encyclical invites us to place a "Spirit Christology" alongside a "logos Christology" and find it a fruitful suggestion.

Let us reflect a moment upon it. In projecting a world, God reveals a longing for creatures who would say "yes" to his love for them. But in so doing, he took the risk that such creatures might say "no" instead. According to the biblical story, prodigal humanity decided to leave the Father's house for a far country. God's love allowed this choice but did not leave it there. The beloved Son who was baptized with the Spirit followed them into the far country to heal the broken relationship and bring them back to union with the triune love. The Spirit empowered the Son to be the fulfillment of what God longs for in the creature and to become the healer of our brokenness. In his vicarious human life, Jesus says "yes" to the Father, experiences the spirit of sonship, and pursues the path which leads him through death to resurrection on our behalf. In Christ, humanity itself is subjected to God and reunited to him as a new humanity (55).

In a Spirit Christology, we "see" Jesus rendering "yes" to God on our behalf and completing a representative journey which brings us back into relationship with God. The true prodigal travels our broken path and replaces our "no" with his "yes," dying in obedience and rising to new life. Redemption comes through solidarity with Christ and his representative journey. Jesus is the gift of God's self-communication and the fulfillment of creation. In him, God gives himself a human heart and communicates the grace of sonship to us humans by the Spirit. Jesus is God's act of healing humanity and providing a new beginning through his recapitulation of our life. Salvation is through Christ's participatory journey accomplished in the power of the Spirit, who enabled him to take the journey and enables us to enter it.

Jesus works atonement not by appeasing an angry God but by taking a representative journey of obedience, on the basis of which the Spirit forms Christ in us and initiates our transformation, breaking the power of sin and death, and leading us to share glory with the risen Lord. We are not saved by an external transaction so much as by a vicarious human journey which leads to union with God and the redemption of creation.

This insight into the Spirit may help us with the proclamation of the gospel. Too often people have been given the distorted idea that God is angry and will not forgive until a third party takes the punishment for them. A Spirit Christology helps correct this portrayal. It was love, not wrath, which brought Jesus, and the cross is an expression of God's desire to save us, not his reluctance. Part of a larger substitution, the cross was the moment of triumph when he accepted the will of the Father, absorbed the evil of humanity, and confronted death itself in order to heal and forgive us. Bringing the Spirit into the narrative of salvation can help us clarify the rationale of atonement and re-evangelize people who have not heard the good news in these appealing accents.

The Holy Spirit in the Life and Mission of His People

As bishop and pastor of a large church, the Pope is also concerned about the power of the Holy Spirit in the life and mission of his people. Therefore, he also wants to celebrate the outpouring of the Spirit on the community which says "yes" to God through Jesus. As Christ's body, the church is filled with the Holy Spirit and can experience the presence of Christ in both sacramental and charismatic life. Often we are required to choose between sacramental and charismatic modes of the real presence of Christ, which is unfortunate because both are valid and should be integrated. I appreciate the encyclical for touching on this two-sided reality.

As a papal document, the encyclical naturally enunciates the ancient catholic tradition concerning the sacramental dimension of church life (89–95) and is it how that Christ comes to the world afresh in the mystery of the church, as she ministers the presence of the risen Lord in the power of the Spirit. As a Protestant myself, I take this point seriously. Many of my fellow Protestants have impoverished themselves by their skepticism about the power of the Spirit in the sacramental life and have discarded ancient liturgies and practices which characterized church life almost from the beginning. As if to mimic the secular rejection of mystery, we have often turned away from the means of grace in which the Spirit renders material things and actions graciously efficacious to faith. I think this is a mistake. The Spirit enables believers to benefit from the bread and the wine, from the preaching, from the fellowship, and from many other signs. We need to take seriously the Catholic tradition on this point. God's presence makes itself felt in all sorts of material ways and God acts among us and meets us through the words and actions of persons. The encyclical points to a recovery of the power of the Holy Spirit in symbols and in the language of the heart.

More briefly, the Pope also refers to the charismatic dimension of the real presence of Christ, speaking of gifts, both hierarchical and charismatic (34). This is certainly another area where expectations of the power of the Spirit need to be expanded among us. As the early church experienced and as modern Pentecostalism has rediscovered, there is divine power in the midst of weakness for the life and mission of the church. There is power to proclaim the gospel and to heal the sick. There is Easter life and the possibility of extraordinary praise, fearless witness, inspired speech, and other signs and wonders. Let us be done with limited expectations in regard to the Spirit and allow him to fall upon us both in our gathering and in our being sent out. In spite of the dangers and risks inherent in charismatic spontaneity, we should be open without restriction to manifestations of the Spirit in and through us.

I think the Pope is acutely conscious of the need to experience the power of the Spirit in the life and mission of the church. I think he would urge us to be less skeptical about the presence of God than we are and have us seek that presence through the Spirit in both the Catholic and charismatic dimensions. To do so would not only enrich our lives, it might greatly facilitate the healing of church divisions, if the sacramental and the charismatic dimensions could be brought back into unity as they were in the first centuries of church life.

Salvation

Another theme in the encyclical which I appreciated looks at salvation from the point of view of the Holy Spirit. It speaks of the Spirit calling us to a growing friendship with God and enabling us to participate in the depths of God's trinitarian life

(47). It speaks of God coming to dwell with us and abide in us and of our sharing in the life of the triune God (17). It says that God gives himself to us by the Spirit and intends to transform us from within (84f). In short, it envisages the goal of salvation as the marriage feast of the Lamb, which symbolizes union and communion in the love of God.

The salvation of a person can be viewed as an awakening to the love of God which the Spirit is pouring out. This in turn results in an experience of sonship and a process of being conformed over a lifetime to the image of the Son, enabling us to love because we now belong to the God who first loved us. Orthodox theologians would call this "divinization," by which they mean we are being restored into the image and likeness of God and reunited to him. I had the impression in the encyclical of the willingness of the Western church to speak the language of the East, which is another ecumenical gain.

The loving Spirit wants to heal individuals, communities, and ultimately the world in this process of salvation. The Spirit is poured out to make us whole, new in body and soul. In this healing is there a third event over and above conversion and sanctification, what many today call "the baptism in the Spirit"? The encyclical does not touch upon this, but would likely take this view of it. The experience of a baptism of the Holy Spirit subsequent to conversion is not best thought of as a second conversion but as a fuller realization in experience of the sonship which marks conversion. It can be viewed as an actualization in experience of the life which was conferred on the believer in baptism and confirmation, a release of the Spirit and a coming into conscious experience of the power of the One who has come.

In creation the trinity throws itself open for the world by sending forth the Spirit—in salvation the world is moved by the Spirit to come back to the Father through the Son, so as to become God's world again.

Pluralism

In a final theme of interest in the encyclical, the Pope finds a way to respond to the issue of religious pluralism by way of the Spirit. He believes that the Spirit can help to make the universality of God's salvific will more credible in a world of many faiths. The encyclical cites a text from the Second Vatican Council reading as follows: "The Holy Spirit in a manner known only to God offers to every man the possibility of being associated with the paschal mystery" (76). This is saying (in the language of evangelical theology) that the Spirit creates an opportunity of salvation among the unevangelized. Regardless of the time and place in which a person lives, it is possible to receive God's offer of salvation because of the Holy Spirit who is active everywhere in the universe.

Although such openness is not original to John Paul or even its reference to the Holy Spirit, this is a particularly strong emphasis of his which he often makes in many speeches. He likes to bring the universal presence and action of the Holy Spirit to bear on this problem. Rather than saying that non-Christian religions as such mediate God's grace as more progressive Catholics like Paul Knitter and even Karl Rahner like to, John Paul focuses on the Spirit of Jesus touching every human heart. The Spirit goes ahead of the mission (prevenience) and the preaching of the gospel and through the Spirit God's love finds a way so that no one will miss an opportunity to be saved. This is an urgent issue for many today and the Pope appeals to the Spirit for an intelligent solution.

Appealing to the Spirit in relation to the unevangelized is an option in the documents of Vatican II (and the Pope cites such a text from *Church in the Modern World*), but it is a rare instance. In John Paul's work, on the other hand, it occurs repeatedly and is his principal theme when speaking about and even to non-Christians. He speaks of the working of the Holy Spirit in non-Christian religious and secular contexts but without recognizing the non-Christian religions themselves as a means of salvation. This is a conservative pope, and he is being cautious at this point, but it seems to me to be a wise caution which avoids the difficulties which more progressive theologians have created by their bolder moves. They have to explain how the very different truth claims made by the various world faiths can possibly serve the salvation Christ has brought, but

John Paul does not, for he simply posits the work of the Spirit on the level of the human heart.

He also makes a contribution to world peace in what he says because of his transparent openness to the world's people. His willingness to recognize God's light and truth among them all is a contribution to good relations and mutual respect. We have come a long way from the days of mutual recrimination and anathemas of a few years ago and this encyclical continues to move us in a positive direction.

This particular theme also illustrates the larger issue of the teaching ministry of the Holy Spirit, of how theological insights can deepen over time in relation to new challenges. In this matter of openness to non-Christians, what the pope says represents a change of attitude on the part of the church and offers (I think) a case study of the Spirit's guiding of the people of God. It may even illustrate the value of having a teaching office in the church. There are topics where (and I speak as a Baptist) one could wish for an authoritative word from above to help people rise above problems which have them trapped. Having a thousand popes is not better than having one.

Celebrating the Holy Spirit

There is great value in the Pope's call to celebrate the Holy Spirit during the coming great jubilee. There is a depth and breadth to his vision, and we are enriched by listening to his words. At the deepest level, I think he is calling us to be assured that, if God's Spirit has given life to the creation and has renewed it through the Incarnation and Pentecost, then we may be confident of receiving grace sufficient for each and every new challenge with which the new millennium will certainly confront us.

Crossing Lessing's Ditch

Michael Williams

Michael Williams is an associate professor of theology at Dordt College in Sioux Center, Iowa, where he teaches courses in such areas as the history of American theological thought, Old Testament literature, the Greek New Testament, and problems in biblical theology.

He earned his Ph.D. from the University of Toronto and has masters degrees from Grand Rapids Baptist Seminary and Harvard Divinity School. Dr. Williams has written a dozen articles and nearly forty reviews in such publications as the *Christian Courier*, the *Grace Theological Journal*, the *Evangelical Journal*, and the *Journal of the Evangelical Theological Society*. In 1995, Dordt Press is publishing his first book, *C.I. Scofield and Lewis Sperry Chafer: American Fundamentalist Gnosticism*.

Last year I attended a philosophical conference on the historicity of the resurrection of Jesus Christ. I knew we were in trouble almost from the beginning, for the discussion throughout centered on the *idea* of the resurrection. While I appreciate the fact that we all think in concepts and that conceptualization is much of what the discipline of philosophy is about, I believe that we too often assume, or fall into the notion, that the reality we are talking about *is* an idea.

At one point in the conference someone asked what status the Christian faith would have if the resurrection of Jesus Christ were not a real-world, historical event. One of the conference coordinators, an older and much published Christian philosopher, admitted that such a state of affairs would indeed be damaging to the faith, although he was not quite sure how, and that we should continue to recommend the Christian faith to people regardless, for even if Christianity lacks any historical underpinnings, it certainly helps people to live better lives. To my absolute amazement, most of the participants nodded their heads in agreement. "Yes," they said, "that is the appropriate response to the question."

Somewhere the question of historicity had just frittered away. They had missed, or dismissed, the issue, the very reason for the conference: to grapple with the historicity of the resurrection of Jesus Christ, its "happenedness" and its significance. People who should have known better had made the critical Enlightenment mistake. I hope that as each one later reflected on that moment that they saw the error. But just for a moment, they seemed, at least to me, to fall into the supposition that it is *ideas*—cut loose from all historical moorings—that fund the Christian faith; that events, historical happenings, are little more than instances or demonstrations of ideas—and apparently unnecessary instances at that.

The hard question in a pluralistic, relativistic world, the hard question since the Enlightenment, the hard question since the very first Easter morning, is this: How can something which claims universal significance—the Christian faith—hinge upon historical events?

This problem has come down to us as the *scandal of particularity,* that an event at one particular locale on the globe can have significance for all people no matter how distant they are in space or time. And not just any event. When we speak of the scandal of particularity, we are talking about events of cosmic import, events that reveal the character of God, that reveal the most fundamental truths about ourselves, the way of salvation, the hope of mankind, and the destiny of all things.

The offensiveness of history was a major plank in the Enlightenment broadside against traditional Christianity. Enlightenment thinkers such as G.E. Lessing (1729–1781) were convinced that history was not a suitable medium for the mediation of absolute and universal truths. The eighteenth-century dictum was that history is too uncertain a ground for religious faith. To the Enlightenment thinker, history is the realm of the contingent and the accidental, not the necessary and universal. The kind of knowledge needed for religion can come only from human reason, it was argued, for reason deals with necessary and universal truths, truths which are clear and rational inferences from first principles, truths which are available to all people regardless of time and space.

Lessing argued that between historical truth and rational truth there stands an unbridgeable gap. "That," he wrote, "is the ugly great ditch which I cannot get across, however often and however earnestly I have tried to make the leap." Lessing believed that the accidental truths of history and the necessary truths of reason are radically different kinds of truth and as such are totally irreconcilable. Truth in the absolute sense cannot be historical, for absolute truth is abstract and timeless, while history is always relative and contingent. No jump can be made between the two.

By seeking a religion which is the necessary inference or deduction of first principles available to a universal human reason, Lessing denounced traditional biblical Christianity as unworthy of belief. He shifted his attention to the natural laws of the external world as proofs of God's existence and to the moral nature of man as evidence of God's moral perfection. Biblical religion became superfluous, if not positively misleading, to the natural religion of Enlightenment rationalism. Some small space for Christianity was maintained, but only insofar as it affirmed or provided instances or illustrations of general moral precepts and rational concepts. Lessing and his cohorts found no need to appeal to history, and thus the narrative quality of the biblical story was disregarded.

Of course, natural religion might legitimately and truthfully tell us *something* about God. If God has made human beings in his image, the correspondence between God and ourselves makes possible a witness to God in the human mind and conscience. If our world is the creation of God, I see no reason to deny John Calvin's contention that "there is not an atom of the universe in which you cannot see some brilliant sparks at least of his glory."

Yet knowledge of God gleaned from the created order and human constitution has real limitations. Were we to accept all the philosophical arguments for the existence of God (e.g., Aquinas' so-called "five ways"), what would we have? Merely the idea that there is Something there, that we are not alone. At most, this god is a "first principle," a "ground of being," that which is "fundamentally basic," an "uncaused cause," or Luke Skywalker's "the force." What we have is not God, but a god-idea, a philosophical construct devoid of substantial particulars. This god is so empty of content that it is finally meaningless for it is compatible with anything whatsoever.[1] Historically, it was but a very short step from the idea of god as a universal rational idea or principle (Hegel) to the notion that god is no more than a projection of the human imagination or a cypher for human ideas (Feuerbach).

Natural religion, of course, was not an invention of the Enlightenment. For many of the philosophers of ancient Greece, God, or the gods, was man writ large, the superlative of positive and the negation of negative human attributes. For the eleventh-century churchman and theologian, Anselm of Canterbury, God was that than which no greater can be conceived. As natural religion was not a new thing with the Enlightenment, neither was the response of biblical orthodoxy. Blaise Pascal put his finger on the problem of natural religion, and at the same time pointed the way toward the true knowledge of God, when he rightly concluded that there is no necessary connection between the god of the philosophers and the God of Abraham, Isaac, and Jacob. One might accept all that human reason says is true about God, and miss the One whom the Creed confesses as God the Father Almighty, maker of heaven and earth. One might accept all the classical arguments for the existence of God and natural religion's definition of God built up by way of supererrogation and the *via negativa*, and never arrive at Sinai or Bethlehem or Golgotha.

And here we return to Lessing's question: How can Christianity claim universal significance when it hinges upon historical events? The answer is really very simple. God is a person. Note that I did not say that God is a human being, but that God is a person. That is the import of Pascal's insight. God is not a theorem, an idea, a notion, a hypothesis, a syllogistic conclusion, or an abstract principle. No person is.

The only way to know another person is to attend to their lives, to the things they say, to the things they do, to the way they relate to others and the world around them. If Napoleon

Bonaparte never said or did anything, if there were no historical references to his words or deeds, if there were no records
of his birth, marriage or death, if no person were able to say
that he went to school with him or bumped into him on the
street or sat next to him at a party, we would have no reason
to believe he ever lived. Without historical action, relationship,
or reference, Napoleon Bonaparte is an abstraction, a vague
idea in the mind. Descriptions of his personal attributes—his
brilliance, ruthlessness, irascibility, determined demeanor—
are all irrelevant, for they would not be embodied in an historical person.

Similarly, when we turn to the Bible we do not find a deity
who is reduced to philosophical propositions, one who ap-
proximates a philosophical problem, one who is a collection
of abstract and impersonal attributes, or one who is the insight
of mystical intuition. We find the One who works in history,
in historical events; and only through those deeds does he
reveal himself, his intentions, his character, his heart. The Bible is fundamentally a story, the story which Christians contend
is the one essentially true story about our world, ourselves, and
God. The Bible tells the story of the cosmos in terms of a
redemptive drama, the chief actor of which is God. The story
centers on his mighty deeds, what he has done, is doing, and
promises yet to do in order to redeem a sin-scarred world. In
Scripture, everything we know about God is related to historical events and relationships. There simply is no other avenue
to a saving knowledge of God. While the creation reflects his
glory, the greatness of his being, it tells us nothing about his
saving intentions or his character, the depths of his heart, the
set of his brow.

The faith of Israel and the faith of Christianity are
founded not in philosophical abstraction but in the acts of God
in human history, in the external and empirical realm of ascer-
tainable events, not some metaphysical timeless heaven. History, not the philosophical abstraction of the human mind, is
the sphere of God's redemption and revelation. Only in history
does God enter into relationships, judge sin, and reconcile the
world to himself in Jesus Christ. As such, the biblical story
speaks of events in the external world. Without the historically

real action of God, the story is no more than a tale, a product of the human imagination. The claims of biblical religion are not funded by mystical experience or private intuition. They are not funded by the necessary inferences of syllogistic reasoning. They are funded by the public, external, and objective deeds by which God discloses himself. If you separate God from his deeds, if you make him no more than a projection of human subjectivity or rationality, what you have is not God at all. You have a hypothesis or a concept. Most certainly, we use concepts—ideas—to think of God, but he is not an idea. Mere ideas do not act. They do not create, covenant, love, command, rule, deliver, or raise the dead. Ideas are concepts held in the minds of persons. Only persons act. G.E. Wright put his finger right on it when he said: "Make abstractions of the ideas, and we divorce them from the reality which brought them forth and gave them relevance. Separate the ideas of God in the Bible from the direct, immediate encounter of him, and we are lost in irrelevant, expansive vacuity."[2]

There is no way to side-step, finesse, or sugar-coat the scandal of historical particularity. The Christian faith is not a religion accessible to every human being apart from reference to particular past events. Christian faith, and the One who is the object of the faith, addresses us in an irreversible and unrepeatable context of events.[3] The ancient Hebrews and the first-century followers of Jesus Christ were aware that historical events must be mediated to us by way of the testimony of witnesses, and further, that their telling of the story is bounded by their perspective—their interpretation. Undaunted by this, they believed that the historical testimony to the acts of God in history is the only kind of knowledge of God that is worth having.[4]

There is no path around but only a path through history.[5] But the norm for the Christian faith must come from beyond history. Meaning is in history, of it, and from it, but its ground, its source, is God himself. The heart of the biblical faith is that God has made himself known in certain, very particular, events in human history, and in very particular human words, not in nature, not in human intuition or mystical experience, and not in human rational processes.[6]

God is known by events, and by special understandings of those events. Not all interpretations of the past are created equal. There is a privileged interpretation of God's redemptive revelation. That is the very purpose of the Bible: to authoritatively mediate the historical acts of God and their significance. That is what the Bible does. It is not the telling of the events which reveals, which saves, but the events. For without the events, the mighty acts of God in the history of our world, there simply is no revelation; there is no redemption. The saving history of Scripture is a history about God. It is a history written by God. And it is a history interpreted by God.

The Bible makes the case over and over again that the God to whom it witnesses is the God of mighty deeds in human history. (This is a particular theme of the book of Exodus.) So shall I. Let me tell you a story, a story from the book of Exodus.[7]

Moses was sent by God to seek the release of Israel from Egyptian thralldom. But things got off to a rather rocky start for Moses when he went to Egypt to carry God's command to Pharoah. Upon hearing the command to release the Israelites, Pharoah told Moses that the instruction of some unknown deity was meaningless to him. There was no reason why the mighty pharoah of Egypt should obey the command of some desert deity. You see, Pharoah knew something about gods. They talk a lot, that is, their priests talk a lot, always trying to get Pharoah to do something: build this, outlaw that, subsidize a third thing. But the deity itself never did anything. It just stood there on the wall, eternally lifeless. Declaring ignorance of Moses' God, Pharoah refused to let Israel go. Further, for Moses' effrontery, for apparently having the time on his Israelite hands to dream up such hooey, Pharoah commanded that Israel must from that day forward make bricks without straw.

At this turn of events, Moses openly charged God with breach of promise. God sent him to seek the release of Israel from bondage. But instead Israel was subjected to harsher oppression. God had not rescued Israel at all. God replies that the promised freedom lies in the future but is sure. Pharoah will indeed let Israel go. God will make things so uncomfortable that Pharoah will not only emancipate Israel, but he will virtually expel them from Egypt. And then God says this to Moses:

> I am Yahweh. I appeared to Abraham, to Isaac and to Jacob as God Almighty, but by my name Yahweh I did not make myself known to them. I also established my covenant with them in the land of Canaan where they lived as aliens. Moreover, I have heard the groaning of the Israelites, whom the Egyptians are enslaving, and I have remembered my covenant. (6:2–5)

God identifies himself here as Yahweh. Most English versions simply translate Yahweh as "The LORD," but that is a mistake. It is a name, not an office or title that is revealed here. Ancient Israel attached great importance to names. A person's name was not a mere vocable. It said something about the person who bore it. A name was a shorthand, a lingual representation of all a person was. It captured something of his or her status, reputation, and character. So this name, the name by which God identifies himself, and gives to Moses to call upon him, is very important.

By announcing his name God reveals his essential character to Moses. He is the One who is there for his people. He is the One who keeps his promises. He is active, dynamic, working in history, entering into relationships, giving and fulfilling promises.[8] This was the great Word to Moses and to that first generation that came through the waters of the Red Sea.

For 430 years the Israelites had seen Pharoah's gods. As the Egyptians' slaves, the Israelites had built the monuments, the tombs, the shrines. They had seen the statues and the paintings on the walls. And they knew, like Pharoah, that gods do not act, they do not speak. In the Exodus, however, they saw and heard something different. Yahweh is different, for Yahweh acts.

Isaiah powerfully makes the case that the issue between the biblical God and the idols of the ancient Near East is not some philosophical question of being but rather one of action and character. In what is certainly the most sarcastic passage in all of Scripture, Isaiah mocks the idols in chapter 44. The carpenter cuts down a cedar or oak. He measures and draws a character on the wood. He roughs out his work with chisels. Should he get tired he will have to rest. Should he hunger, he cuts off a portion of the tree and uses it for cooking fuel to bake his bread. Late in the day the weather turns foul and cool.

He cuts off another part of the tree to build a fire for warmth. From what is left he carves his own likeness, man in all his awesome glory. He bows down to it and worships. He prays to it and says, "Save me; you are my god."

Existence, you see, is not the issue. Of course the gods exist. Man makes them. He can hold his idol in his hand. The issue is action, person, character. The false god of the idol-maker is blind; it sees nothing. It can speak no word that man does not first give it. It is an impotent dead thing.

What sets Yahweh apart from the idols is that he is most assuredly not a projection of human intellect or subjectivity. The name Yahweh is a declaration that God can only be grasped and understood by his acts and words. Only *his* action reveals his presence and character. Man cannot discover it or forget it. Israel can know God and learn of his true nature only through his acts of redemption. Israel can understand who God is only by what he did on her behalf. The giving of his name is the promise of his personal presence. "I am your God. I am with you. I am here for you." This God cannot be known coldly, speculatively, or abstractly. Knowing God is not a question of philosophical definitions of essence or being. He can only be known as all persons are known: in the existentially relevant warp-and-woof of historical existence.[9]

To prove his case, to establish his intent to be Moses' God, Yahweh makes a series of promises to Moses. "I will bring you out," Yahweh says first; then, "I will free you from being slaves, I will be redeem you, I will take you as my people, I will be your God, I will bring you to the land I swore to give to Abraham, and I will give it to you as a possession." The litany of seven promises is tied up as with a bow in the litany, "I am Yahweh." Four times God repeats that declaration, as if to make absolutely sure that Moses knows who he is dealing with. "I, Yahweh, promise you." He is not deity in general or god in the abstract. He is a specific God, a distinctive God, a God who cannot be confused with idols of wood or of mind. He speaks, and he keeps his word by his action: "The name Yahweh functions as a guarantee that the reality of God stands behind the promise and will execute its fulfillment."[10]

There are many gods. In fact, John Calvin spoke of fallen

man as a virtual idol-factory. As a worshipping creature, man makes the gods he wants for himself. He might carve his idol from stone or wood, or cast it in metal. He might make his race or his political ideology or his wealth his god. But he himself has made the god. But not Yahweh. Yahweh is the maker of all; he is not the thing made. To be Creator is one thing; to be creature is quite another.

To believe in the biblical God, to believe in Yahweh, is not merely to be convinced of the existence of some vague supreme being. Nor is it to accept the generic deity of classical liberalism. To believe in Yahweh is to recognize the God who creates, who makes promises, and who acts in history to fulfill his promise. To believe in Yahweh is to believe in a *particular* deity. To believe in Yahweh is not merely to reject atheism. Any god is not better than no god. Nor is it merely to refuse to worship anything which is not him. The First Commandment, "You shall have no other gods before me," is not only a commandment of exclusion; it is also a commandment of exclusivity (me alone will you worship). All that is not God; is creaturely, including our notions of God. To worship the creature is idolatry and superstition.

The Bible gives neither an abstract definition of God nor a philosophical proof of his existence. His mighty deeds are the proof of Yahweh's presence. The goal of Yahweh's redemptive activity is that men see his works, believe his promise, and know that he is God, the only God worthy of worship. By visible events, demonstrable validations of his power and intentions, by fulfilling his promises, God acted in such a way that his revelation of himself cannot be written off as a mere mental exercise, as pious imagination, or as the vain hope of a debased slave people.

Over and over again in Exodus runs the refrain that God will redeem Israel in such a way that Israel will know that he is Yahweh the keeper of promise, that Egypt will know that he is Yahweh the God of Israel (e.g., 6:7; 7:5, 18; 9:24, 29). "I am Yahweh," God declares to Moses, as if to say, "if you want to know who I am, watch me work."[11]

Lessing contended that because history concerns unique,

unrepeatable events, it cannot serve to demonstrate truth. Since history cannot be rationalistically demonstrated, nothing can be demonstrated by history. Lessing was able to make such a claim about the alleged irrelevance of historical events because of his commitment to absolute truth in the deductive or mathematical mode, truths supposedly available to all, regardless of historical or geographical context. For God to qualify as such a truth, God would have to be reduced to a mathematical axiom or a necessary inference of Aristotelian class logic. In other words, God would have to be impersonal. God would have to be something other than God and less than God. He, or I should say "it," would be nothing more than the god of Enlightenment deism.

Lessing has moved in a direction which is the exact counter to the biblical revelation. Where Lessing has impersonalized God, the biblical story moves towards ever fuller and more complete levels of personalization, of particularity. Let me illustrate. If I were to say that I knew my wife just as well during our first year of marriage as I do now over twenty years later, you would have every right to ask if I had been awake during the ensuing twenty-one years. We learn of the existence of people upon meeting them or hearing about them or reading about them, but we come to know them only by watching them over a period of time. After all, *knowing* and *knowing about* are quite different things. If you had asked me about Jackie Williams in 1974, I could have told you about some of her personal habits, tastes, and commitments. Ask me about her today, and I can tell you how she will act in particular situations; I can tell you of her integrity; I can tell you what kind of mother she has become; I can tell you how she has found the grace to be long-suffering and loving to a man who was for far too many years a professional student; I can tell you of a woman who knows me far better than I am always comfortable with; I can tell you a love story. Knowing another person is fundamentally an historical affair. It takes time. It takes action. It takes personal commitment.

That is how it is with all persons, and God; his name says that about him. "Watch as I prove my character over and over again, keeping faith, establishing my reputation, defending it, walking with my people, making promises, and fulfilling my words." To proclaim his name is to describe his character.

When the promised deliverance was accomplished in the liberation of Israel from Egypt, God took a major step in vindicating himself and disclosing his character to men. Israel no longer needed to speculate about the existence and problematic nature of the gods. Her God, Yahweh, the One who is there for his people, is active in history. He reveals himself in word and deed. In Moses' song by the sea in Exodus 15 we read:

> I will sing to Yahweh, for he is highly exalted.
> The horse and its rider he has hurled into the sea.
> Yahweh is my strength and my song; he has become my salvation.
> He is my God, and I will praise him, my father's God,
>   and I will exalt him.
>
> Yahweh is a warrior; Yahweh is his name.
> Pharoah's chariots and his army he has hurled into the sea.
> The best of Pharoah's officers are drowned in the Red Sea....
>
> Who among the gods is like you, O Yahweh?
> Who is like you—majestic in holiness, awesome in glory,
>   working wonders?
> You stretched out your right hand and the earth swallowed them.
> (Exodus 15:1–4, 11–12)

The promise inherent in the name Yahweh was fulfilled in the historical events of the Exodus from Egypt. God's reputation, bound up as it was with the destiny of Israel, was vindicated. This God is not known in abstract timeless propositions about his being, but through concrete, external events. He is known by very specific events, by the roles he plays within the ongoing life of his people. He is the King of creation, the Shepherd of his people, the Lawgiver, Judge, Savior, Husband, and Father of Israel. *He is the incomparable God of power and action.* Next to him, the little tinker-toy gods of the ancient Near Eastern pantheon of deities are nothing more than sticks fit only for cooking fuel. Next to him, the god of natural religion is too insubstantial to be real, a mere concept, perhaps merely a dream.

By delivering Israel from Pharoah, God established his character as a warrior. It might jar modern, sanitized, politically correct, and confessionally pluralistic sensibilities to speak of God this way, but the ancients knew what warriors were and did. The warrior calls up images of struggle, strife, combat, and absolute commitment. The image is thoroughly personal and relational. It mattered, and it mattered urgently, whether the warrior was for you or against you. A warrior takes sides. The warrior stands for something, for someone, and with someone. The warrior enlists in a cause and places himself and his reputation in harm's way. The warrior is never a casual or disinterested observer, never an abstraction.

The different roles God plays in history always lead us to use language which is appropriate for human beings. But because God is not a human being, it has been common within the theological tradition, especially since the Enlightenment, to say that any speaking about God as one would a human being is metaphorical or analogical. God is not actually a warrior or king or judge; he merely appears to be something like a warrior, king, or judge. But this is to confuse the order of knowing with the order of being. A warrior is one who wages war. A king is a person who exercises a sovereignty over a domain. A judge is a person who makes critical decisions about guilt and innocence, culpability and responsibility, truth and falsehood. God does these things. As one who makes war, rules, and judges, he is warrior, ruler, judge. He is not a metaphor; his actions are not metaphorical; and describing him in these very concrete terms is not metaphorical. We have creaturely, historical experience of such persons in the order of knowing. Our knowing is analogical to be sure. We organize our knowledge and experience of the new in terms of what is already known. Once we have built up an experiential referent for the word "sculptor," and then are introduced to Michelangelo (either by meeting him personally and watching him work or by viewing his David), we do not say that Michelangelo is somehow sculptor-like, as if in reality he is not a sculptor. We see that he has the properties of a sculptor (he sculpts: he carves, chisels, welds, and molds) and thus is a sculptor.[12]

What we have in the biblical testimony of God in his speaking and acting are not metaphors but accommodations, adaptations to the needs of the situation and the capacities of the human recipients. Finally, God vastly transcends our capacities of language, thought, and imagination, but in his historical self-disclosure God comes to us, meeting us on our creaturely, contextual level. What is crucially important about God's accomodated historical self-disclosure is not only that he is more than that disclosure of his person, but also that he is never less than that disclosure.

Alongside of Israel being delivered out of Egypt and passing through the Red Sea by the hand of God, the book of Exodus is famous in most minds for its recording of the events at Sinai, most notable of which is the giving of the law. Immediately prior to the declaration of the Ten Commandments, God identified himself to Israel, saying: "I am Yahweh your God, who brought you out of Egypt, out of the land of slavery." (Exo.20:1) This statement is a crucial piece of the covenant document of Exodus 20 and following. Upon entering into an obligatory relationship with a subordinate or vassal, the sovereign would cite his past dealings with the vassal by recounting the ways he had protected or aided the vassal in the past. This recounting of the sovereign's historical faithfulness would then stand as the guarantee of his protection and assistance in the ensuing relationship. If the recorded specific instances of the sovereign's gracious dealings with the vassal were not true, then there would be no ground of relationship, and the vassal would have no good reason to comply with the stipulations of the contract, the *covenant*.[13]

The giving of the law at Sinai was dependent on the fact of God's deliverance of Israel out of Egypt. Sidney Greidanus is right when he insists that the formalized introduction to the covenant, the *historical prologue,* must list "genuine historical occurences." If it does not, "it defeats its own purpose of placing the vassal in a position of obligation."[14] The giving of the law required the historical referent of the Exodus. In the telling of the Israelites' exodus out of Egypt, the event is nonnegotiable because it is the event itself that is the message.

In effect, the message of Exodus 20:1 is this: "I have delivered you. I have proven myself to be Yahweh, your God. If I did not deliver you, you have no reason to worship me or obey me. If I did not keep my word, there is no reason to trust me in the future. But, behold, you are not in Egypt anymore." By citing his own historical action, God is giving Israel a reason, an historical, evidentiary reason why they should obey the covenantal stipulations of the law.[15]

God is an evidentialist. Throughout the biblical story he declares himself a doer of deeds, not a deduction, not a mystic's ecstacy. Whenever he comes to them, God gives his people a history lesson. History makes our relationship with God possible. History sustains the life of faith. When God introduces himself at Sinai, he does not say that he is the God who lives within their subjectivity or even their intellect. He says that he is the God of concrete historical deeds. He is the God of their fathers, the God of Abraham, of Isaac, and of Jacob. That is the refrain throughout the story. The evidentialist point is this: If he was not there, if he was not the God of the patriarchs, if he did not rescue Israel out of Egypt, there is simply no reason to believe in him. There is no reason to expect that he is here now. Yahweh is preeminently the God of history. As Richard Lints puts it, Yahweh "was the God who acted on the plane of history. And he was constantly reminding Israel that, as he had acted in the past, so he would continue to act in the future. God had always been the primary actor on the stage of history, shaping that history according to his will, and he would continue to do so."[16]

As the historical prologue of the law at Sinai makes plain, the past is the key to the present. Our deductions may be our conveniences. Our ecstatic religious experiences may have no referent outside of our own subjectivity. God is finally, and most fully, known by his self-disclosed and self-interpreted ways in human history. Yet this history is not the naively or allegedly objective and disinterested history of nineteenth-century liberal historiography. To know Yahweh, one must enter the

story. One must go backward in order to go forward.[17] One
finds not only the identity of God there, but one's own identity
as well. And that is exactly what we see in the biblical confes-
sions of God. Deuteronomy 26:5–9 is often called the *little
credo,* the little confession. This text functioned for the Old
Testament community of faith much like the Apostles' Creed
functions for us in the New Testament era. The credo was a
declaration of praise for God's mighty deeds. The faithful Hebrews were instructed to bring their offerings to the priest and
to declare their gratitude to God by publicly rehearsing the
great things Yahweh had done for them and their ancestors:

> My father was a wandering Aramean, and he went down into
> Egypt with a few people and lived there and became a great
> nation, powerful and numerous. But the Egyptians mistreated
> us and made us suffer, putting us to hard labor. Then we cried
> out to Yahweh, the God of our fathers, and Yahweh heard our
> voice and saw our misery, toil, and oppression. So Yahweh
> brought us out of Egypt with a mighty hand and an outstretched
> arm, with terror and with miraculous signs and wonders.

There are no abstract definitions of attributes here, no deductions of what sort of being God must be, no arguments about
the existence of God. What there is is an identification of
Yahweh as the Savior of his people.

Biblical confession is a recitation of the redemptive intent
and actions of God.[18] Each generation, "your children and
their children after them," was to be taught what God had
done. They were to know this history because it was both their
history and the key to their identity and because it was through
this history that they would learn about the God who called
them.

The Reformation era humanist and biblical scholar, Eras-
mus of Rotterdam, once said that so long as a man remains
silent he remains a mystery. The same is true of God. Without
his speaking and acting, his intentions, character, and personality will ever remain unknown. But the biblical story is about
God speaking and acting. And speaking and acting in such a
way that he becomes ever more personal, that his ways become
ever more concrete. The biblical story is not about the accumu-

lation of data, about some metaphysical realm of absolute truth and beauty. The biblical story is not about the ascent of man in the mystical negation of history and creational reality. The biblical story is about the descent of God. It is about God coming to earth, making his will and his person known in man's historical existence. From its very beginnings, the biblical story is about the God who "so loved the world" as to create it, act upon and within it, and ultimately to become part of it. God does just that in Jesus Christ.

God has left his footprints in history most clearly and most fully in Jesus Christ. Whatever vague or muddled ideas that man has about the character and nature of God are decisively addressed and corrected in God's coming in the flesh of Jesus of Nazareth. God is now utterly distinctive and absolutely particular. With the birth of Jesus, the incarnation, the enfleshment of God, Yahweh is now christologically disclosed and defined. All that was represented in the Old Testament name Yahweh is now found in the promise of Jesus' name: the LORD saves. To say *Yahweh* was, for the Hebrew, to be reminded of the Exodus. And to say *Jesus* is, for the Christian, to be reminded of the cross.

A Christ-idea can do no more than an abstract definition of God. The person who has Christian faith is a believer in the historical Jesus, the one who was God come in the flesh, who was crucified under Pontius Pilate, and rose again from the dead.[19] I like the way Hillsdale College Director of Christian Studies Michael Bauman puts it: While our understanding of Christ "must not be merely historical, it must be historical at least and historical always."[20] A Jesus idea can save no one. But Jesus can. The light of the world and the hope of sinners is not found in the seer's dream or the philosopher's idea. God's action in history remains the starting point. George Ladd was exactly right: "Existential impact results only from historical event."[21] If God is God, he acts decisively and definitively in history.

Without the historical reality of Jesus walking the dusty roads of Palestine, of suffering and dying for the sins of mankind, of rising from the dead, the gospel message cannot save.

"Central to the New Testament is the fact that it is not the message itself which saves men and women but the historical event of Jesus' life, death, and resurrection."[22]

Christianity is an historical religion, wedded to the historical self-disclosure of God. And the acme of that disclosure is the biblical affirmation that the Word became flesh. God himself came to earth and entered into man's empirical reality so completely that the Gospel of John can say that to see Jesus is to see the human face of God (John 1:18). God moves toward particularity in Christ, toward personal disclosure. This is the essence of Christianity. In a much quoted passage, F.F. Bruce suggests that to miss the historical grounding of the gospel in the this-worldly life, death, and resurrection of Christ is to miss the very message:

> For the Christian gospel is not primarily a code of ethics or a metaphysical system; it is first and foremost good news, and as such it was proclaimed by its earliest preachers.... And this good news is intimately bound up with the historical order, for it tells how for the world's redemption God entered history, the eternal came into time, the kingdom of heaven invaded the realm of earth, in the great events of the incarnation, crucifixion and resurrection of Jesus the Christ.[23]

No other world religion stakes its life on the external historical facticity of its claims as tenaciously as does Christianity. The Christian revelation does not come via speculations or intuitions, but rather through a history which is objective and external to the human subject. Before King Agrippa, Paul defended the historical facticity of Christ's fulfillment of Old Testament promise: "I am speaking the sober truth. For the king knows about these things, and to him I speak freely; for I am persuaded that none of these things has escaped his notice, for this was not done in a corner" (Acts 26:25–26). Peter's sermon at Pentecost contains these significant words: "Men of Israel, hear these words: Jesus of Nazareth, a man attested to you by God with mighty works and wonders and signs which God did through him in your midst, as you yourselves know." (Acts 2:22)

Bishop Newbigen is certainly correct when he states that "the whole of Christian teaching would fall to the ground if it were the case that the life, death, and resurrection of Jesus were not events in real history but stories told to illustrate truths which are valid apart from these happenings."[24] Only the Christian religion dares to make such a bold assertion as Paul's: "If Christ has not been raised, our preaching is useless and so is your faith." It's as simple as this: If God did not deliver Israel out of Egypt, if he did not raise Jesus from the grave, we have no reason to believe, no right to believe, that he will act now or in the future. Without its historical foundations, the Christian faith and the biblical witness to a God who works in history and is known by that activity, loses all point and merely evaporates. My students sometimes complain: "It is enough that Jesus lives in my heart." To which I reply: "If he did not enter this earthly life at Bethlehem, if he did not die at Calvary, if he was not in the upper room on the Easter evening raised to life, what you have is heartburn and pipe dreams."

If history is as irrelevant and as truly boring as the modern college freshman comes to school thinking, it is news to God. Everything about the biblical faith is historical. The Bible is an event-centered revelation. It communicates its message in terms of, in the midst of, and through the mediation of historical events. Rather than making its appeal in terms of universal propositions about being or God's immediate relevance to a private religious sojourn, Scripture proclaims its message in terms of its pattern of divine action in fulfillment of promise and the historical recountings of promises kept.

Far from seeking release from temporality or historicity, far from presenting a universalized story or one easily transportable into some other time, the Bible insists upon the facts of history and historical particularity. The language of Scripture does not theorize, idealize, allegorize, speculate, or deduce. Quite the contrary, it is the language of depiction, of events, of history. One relates to such language, to such events, to the God who discloses himself there, not by dehistorical moralization, subjectivist internalization, or philosophical depersonalization, but by participation in the redemptive-historical community which carries the story.

The only God worthy of worship is the One who keeps his promises. In the Exodus, he kept the promise made long before to the patriarchs that he would covenant a people into existence. In the resurrection of Jesus from the dead, God paid off on a promise that was even more ancient, a promise that was also the divine declaration of war against the kingdom of Satan. "Satan, you will bruise the heel of my seed, but you will have precious little time to gloat over your supposed victory. For as sure as I am Yahweh, he will crush your head."

That is what the drama of redemption is about finally, God's faithfulness to his promise. When a student once asked me why I expected the class to know something about the history of the Old Testament, I replied that it was the only way to learn of the faithfulness of God, a fundamental element of God's character. The student's rejoiner, however serious, was deeply flawed. He said, in effect: "If that's all that it's about, just attach a note to the beginning of Matthew saying 'God is faithful.'" But we do not learn of the integrity of another person by merely being told of his virtues. It requires repeated attestation in event, witness, and record. It requires the testing of circumstance. It has to be proven in the light of history over time, and the longer the better.

The scandal of particularity cannot be side-stepped. I suspect that the real scandal is not some polite philosophical concern for universality, but rather the incorrigibility of the God of biblical revelation. Persons cannot be manhandled the way ideas can. When an idea does not fit we simply change it, knock off an edge here, a burr there. But people will not be so easily manipulated. The biblical God offends us with his very over-againstness. Where the deities of the seer and the philosopher are decidedly underwhelming in their lack of edges and burrs, the God who discloses his personality and will in biblical revelation comes to us in a concrete history which refuses to bend to our will.[25] That history refuses to corroborate our decision about God or the depths of our pious passion because it has nothing to do with religious imagination, inner experience, or deductive reasonings. The story is not ours to cast in our image because it is about the decision of God and Christ's passion. It is not God's existence which is the question in the biblical drama but ours.[26]

Rejecting the realm of history as the accidental and the

contingent, G.E. Lessing sought a confessional truth which was the necessary inference of axiomatic principles. He missed the necessity in the historical self-disclosure of God. We might call it the necessity of character. Yahweh is just the sort of God who, upon finding the man and the woman hiding in shame in the garden, promises to redeem his fallen creation. He is just the sort of God who would refuse to surrender his creation to chaos. It is thoroughly consistent with his character to redeem a people and take them to himself. It was the natural thing for him to do to send his own Son to the cross and therein redeem a sin-sick world. It was necessary, for he could have done no other and remained Yahweh, God the Father Almighty, maker of heaven and earth.

Notes

1. Strangely, the deity of natural religion is even compatible with the idea that the cosmos is divine, that god is "being itself" or the "depth of being." Long before the New Age phenomenon came on the scene, John Warwick Montgomery rightly wrote that conceiving of god pantheistically leaves us no reason to talk about god at all, since it tells us nothing more than we knew before, namely, that the universe exists. To say that the universe is divine is not to say anything of real significance. *The Suicide of Christian Theology* (Minneapolis: Bethany Fellowship, 1970).

2. G.E. Wright, *The Challenge of Israel's Faith* (Chicago: University of Chicago, 1944), 29.

3. See Alan Richardson, *History Sacred and Profane* (London: SCM, 1964), 210.

4. M.C. Smit writes: "Meaning is *in* history, is *of* history, arises *from* history. This implies, however, that man seeks meaning in something which itself is limited, fleeting, finite, relative, which is to say in something that does not have the ground of its existence in itself." *Writings on God and History*, Vol. 1, trans. by Herbert Donald Morton (Jordan Station, Ontario: Wedge, 1987), 196.

5. Ibid., 197.

6. H. Berkhof, "God in Nature and History," in *God, History, and Historians*, edited by C.T. McIntire (New York: Oxford University Press, 1977), 295.

7. I choose to tell the story through the book of Exodus because the revelational pattern of event as the demonstration of divine presence, the vindication of God's deity, really begins in the Exodus story. Moses understood the purpose of the plagues against Egypt as overt, empirical, historical demonstrations of divine power, a power that would lead Pharoah to acknowledge the lordship of Yahweh and thus release the captive Israelites from bondage.

8. See Brevard Childs, *Old Testament Theology in a Canonical Context* (Philadelphia: Fortress, 1985), 39; Childs, *The Book of Exodus* (Philadelphia: Westminster, 1974), 114; R. Alan Cole, *Exodus* (London: InterVarsity, 1973), 69–70; John I. Durham, *Exodus* (Waco, Texas: Word, 1987), 38–39.

9. Calvin held that we never know God in the abstract, as he is in himself (*ad intra*), but only as he comes to us in his revelation of himself (*ad extra*). Our knowledge of God is shaped by, and comes in terms of, "the down-to-earth, experiential concreteness of the biblical narrative." In Gordon Spykman, *Reformational Theology: A New Paradigm for Doing Dogmatics* (Grand Rapids: Eerdmans, 1992), 93.

10. Childs, *The Book of Exodus*, 115.

11. To confess God as Yahweh, the covenant God of promise, is roughly equivalent to the Apostles' Creed confession of "God the Father Almighty." As father, God calls a people into familial relationship. As almighty, he is able to fulfill his fatherly intent.

12. Regarding the anthropomorphic revelations of God in Scripture, G.E. Wright (op. cit., 66–67) makes a lot of sense when he claims that before we dismiss that language as unsophisticated or unduly phenomenological we must keep in mind that Israel's "God was no abstract idea or principle. He was a living, active, powerful God. Hence anthropomorphism in Old Testament religion was the *very reason* for its dynamic and virile character. It is a question, therefore, whether such a view is not even more 'advanced' than some modern definitions of God as a principle of integration, the sum of human ideals, or the vital energy regulating and ordering matter. . . . As long as we are human (and there seems small chance of our becoming gods), we must use human categories to describe the Divine Being. *There is little in an abstract principle which can stir the emotions or strike at the will. We are forced, therefore, to make use of such concrete terms as may make God appear to*

be what what he is—a living, compelling, sovereign reality." (emphasis mine)

13. Sidney Greidanus, *The Modern Preacher and the Ancient Text* (Grand Rapids: Eerdmans, 1988), 94.

14. Ibid., 195.

15. See Wright, 58–63, for an excellent discussion of the divine name as the foundation of the moral law of Israel.

16. Richard Lints, *The Fabric of Theology: A Prolegomenon to Evangelical Theology* (Grand Rapids: Eerdmans, 1993), 263.

17. Ibid., 276, 316. Cf. David Wells, *No Place for Truth: Or Whatever Happened to Evangelical Theology?* (Grand Rapids: Eerdmans, 1993), 259.

18. G.E. Wright, *The God Who Acts: Biblical Theology as Recital* (London: SCM, 1952), 38, claims that biblical confession is "first and foremost a theology of recital, in which Biblical man confesses his faith by reciting the formative elements of his history as the redemptive handiwork of God. The realism of the Bible consists in its close attention to the facts of history and of tradition because these facts are the facts of God."

19. I. Howard Marshall, *I Believe in the Historical Jesus* (Grand Rapids: Eerdmans, 1977), 84.

20. Michael Rauman, unpublished manuscript, 87.

21. George Ladd, *The Pattern of New Testament Truth* (Grand Rapids: Eerdmans, 1968), 63.

22. Nigel Scotland, *Can We Trust the Gospels?* (Exeter: Paternoster, 1979), 48.

23. F.F. Bruce, *The New Testament Documents: Are They Reliable?* (Grand Rapids: Eerdmans, 5th ed., 1978 [1960]), 7–8. Cf. R.T. Brookes, *Communicating Conviction* (London: Epworth, 1983), 50: "An incarnational faith must rest on real events. The hard documentary element in the Christian story must be told for what it is—and received for what it is."

24. Bishop Newbigen, *The Gospel in a Pluralist Society* (Grand Rapids: Eerdmans, 1989), 66.

25. Eliezer Berkovits, *God, Man, and History: A Jewish Interpretation* (Middle Village: Jonathan David, 1959), 12–15. Berkovits appropriately writes: "It is commonplace to say that biblical religion

knows of no speculative roots for God's existence. It is one of the surprising features of the Bible that nowhere does it make the slightest attempt to prove rationally that there is a God. Now, this is not all due to the naive piety of the biblical narrative—the Bible is anything but a book of naivety—but to the very essence of religion. Whether God's existence may be proved rationally or not is of little interest to religion. . . . [I]t is possible for man to entertain extremely exalted philosophical opinions concerning God and yet—just because of such opinion—reject religion proper. . . . The foundation of religion is not the affirmation that God is, but that God is concerned with man and the world; that, having created the world, He has not abandoned it. . . . The foundation of biblical religion, therefore, is not an idea but an event which may be called the encounter of God and man."

26. In a wonderful paragraph in *No Place for Truth* (279), David Wells declares: "The Bible is not a remarkable illustration of what we have already heard within ourselves; it is a remarkable discovery of what we have not and cannot hear within ourselves. Thus, our inward sense of God and our intuitions about meaning are irrelevant in our effort to differentiate biblical truth from pagan belief. It is how we apply ourselves to learn what God has disclosed of himself in a realm outside of ourselves that is important. And unless we steadfastly maintain this distinction in the face of the modern pressures to destroy it, we will soon find that we are using the Bible merely to corroborate the validity of what we have already found within our own religious consciousness— which is another way of saying that we are putting ourselves in place of the Bible. It is another way of asserting the old paganism. When that happens, theology is irredeemably reduced to autobiography, and preaching degenerates into mere storytelling."

Reclaiming Stolen Property: The Liberal Church Crisis and the Young Fogeys

Thomas C. Oden

Thomas C. Oden is the Henry Anson Buttz Professor of Theology and Ethics
at the Theological School and Graduate School of Drew University in Madison, New Jersey. With a Ph.D. from Yale University, he has taught at universities throughout the U.S. as well as in Germany, Italy, and Russia.

From 1983 to 1991, he was the host of a popular New Jersey television
program called *Authors.* Currently, he is a senior editor of *Christianity Today*
and serves on the editorial board of the *Journal of Pastoral Care,* the *Journal of
Christian Counseling,* and Zondervan's academic books division. He also works
with numerous pastoral, hospital, and student groups.

Dr. Oden has edited numerous books and has written twenty-four of
his own, including *The Fathers on Christian Doctrine, The Transforming Power of
Grace, Life in the Spirit, The Living God, Agenda for Theology: Recovering Christian
Roots, Conscience and Dividends,* and *The Crisis of the World and the Word of God.*
His latest works are *Requiem: A Lament in Three Movements* and *Corrective Love:
The Power of Communion Discipline.*

An interloper who steals property must be caught and
fairly charged as a requirement of justice. Thinly disguised
atheism and neo-paganism are now cocky interlopers in liberated church circles. We have witnessed the theft of church
property by forces alien and inimical to the Apostolic Tradition. The stolen property must be reclaimed and the thieves
brought to justice.

The momentous sea change reversal elections of November 1994 represented a defining turning point in American
consciousness. In the light of this decisive new context—regardless of whether one might have wept or cheered over its
political consequences—it is now a fitting time to speak can-

didly about the current crisis of mainline or old-line liberal Protestantism. Is there, as some have argued, only a brief window of opportunity to reclaim liberal Protestantism to the faith of classic Christianity? Is it collapsing from within? Is it redeemable?

By mainline Protestantism, I mean those heirs of Luther, Calvin, Cranmer, Wesley, and Edwards whose leadership has been deeply implicated for decades in romantic social activism and bureaucratic ecumenism—Methodist social perfectionists who have forgotten Wesley's treatise on original sin, guilt laden, works-righteous Presbyterians, heirs of the Congregationalist tradition who have become megachurch bureaucrats, and forgetful, historical, permissive Episcopalians. In each of these communions there is an active and growing dissenting movement, such as the Confessing Movement within the United Methodist Church, which in only the first few months of volunteer leadership gained the support of over six thousand local church official boards. It is time not merely to kindle angry new condemnatory grievances, but to ask how God the Spirit is calling the faithful within all these communions to work constructively together toward the practical repossession of renegade church bureaucracies and liberated elites. The quality of this discussion on the future of mainline Protestant bureaucracies has potentially fate-laden relevance for Catholic, Orthodox and Evangelical traditions as well.

The compelling practical issue is: Can advocates of classic Christianity (among them a considerable cultural variety of doctrinally orthodox and moral traditionalists, evangelicals and shell-shocked moderates, and liturgical conservatives and institutional centrists) come together cooperatively to form a solid accord with a trusted and viable agenda for recapturing classic Christian teaching and ecclesiastical leadership in the mainline? Can a trajectory be set that will not slide down the slippery slope toward resentment and reactionary defensiveness? Can those who remain dedicated to classic Christian teaching find a credible voice to challenge the long dominant hegemony of liberal romanticists, subjectivists, sentimentalists, and pantheists? Can loyal stay-inners cope with despairing temptations to walk away and abandon the struggle?

A massive moral crisis is facing liberal church leadership, its seminaries, bureaucracies, and local churches. It is time to reconceive a common vision sharable by classical centrists and traditionalists for repossession of our church institutions, and to set feasible goals for the reeducation and rehabilitation of a tradition-deprived church. How can we belatedly reclaim our identity, our institutions, our academies, our mission?

Luther had ninety-five theses, Kierkegaard only one (that New Testament Christianity does not exist in culturally accommodative Denmark). I am less dismal than Kierkegaard and less lavish the Luther, since I have honed my concise Hillsdale theses down to less than a couple dozen paragraphs.

The following modest theses are offered, not as if fully argued, but to be nailed up for discussion, or at least tacked symbolically onto the academic computer bulletin board, as indicative of defensible directions that invite further development. They reveal an insider's view of the acute predicament of the liberal church amid this cultural crisis, with special reference to the arena of theological education. I am pouring out my heart about a broken love affair. Having pledged my life to serve Protestant theological education, I now find the task extremely difficult to accomplish within present parameters. But, by grace the parameters can be reconfigured.

What is the decisive theological issue of the church amid proximate temporary apostasy? I want to focus first on the doctrinal issue that most deeply affects our moral courage and ability to relate to this cultural opportunity. It might surprise some that of all possible theological points that need to be explored, I chose to focus on an oft-neglected theme, yet familiar to Augustine, Aquinas, Calvin, and Cranmer: the "indefectibility" of the church. My opening thesis is: *The one, holy, universal church is promised imperishable continuance, even if particular churches or local bodies or denominations may languish, falter, or atrophy.*

The church's future is finally left, not to human willing or chance, but to grace. Many branches of the seasonally changing vine may drop off in the recurring autumns of cul-

tural histories or become dysfunctional or atrophy, but the
church as the Body of Christ will be preserved till the end of
the age. The destiny of the church is eternally secure. Though
individual believers may come to shipwreck, and even whole
communities may lose their bearings during particular periods
of demonic confusion and moral debacle, the church will be
sheltered and sustained by grace until the end (John 16:6, 13).
God will not be left without witnesses in the world (Acts 14:17).
"One Holy Christian church will be and remain forever"
(*Augsburg Confession*, Art. VII). According to my own church's
traditional Order for Receiving Persons into the Church: "The
Church is of God, and will be preserved to the end of time, for
the promotion of his worship and the due administration of
his Word and Sacraments, the maintenance of Christian Fellowship and discipline, the edification of believers, and the
conversion of the world. All of every age and station, stand in
need of the means of grace which it alone supplies." This is a
passage once known by heart among any pastor of my tradition.

Meanwhile the church continues to be vulnerable to those
hazards that accompany historical existence generally. Thus a
second classic thesis deserves further rediscovery and refinement: *The Holy Spirit does not abandon the ever-formative living
Christian tradition amid these earthly struggles, but supplies that grace
of perseverance by which the church is enabled to remain Christ's living
body even while being challenged by infirmities, forgetfulness, heresy,
apostasy, persecution, and schism.* It is promised that the church
will be preserved to "proclaim the Lord's death until he comes"
(1 Cor. 11:26). Against the church, Jesus declared in Matthew's
gospel: "The gates of hell shall not prevail" (16:18, KJV; cf.
Luke 1:33; 1 Tim. 3:15). This means that the church will never
decline into total forgetfulness, since guided by the Spirit who
promises always to accompany the faithful (John 14:16; Matt
23:20). Even when short-term ecclesiastical management fails
pathetically in accountability, the church, insofar as empowered by the Spirit, does not ever fall entirely away from the
living Lord or from the truth of faith or into irretrievable error.

She is preserved by grace, not by human craft or strategic cleverness (Matt. 7:25).

This awakens a third promising thesis to be explored: *Despite temporary, real, and devastating apostasies, it is unthinkable that God would allow the church finally to become absolutely and continuously apostate or to lose all touch with the righteousness which Christ has once and for all bestowed upon her.* "For you have been born again, not of perishable seed, but of imperishable, through the living and enduring Word of God. For 'all men are like grass,'" but "'the word of the Lord stands forever.' And this is the word that was preached to you" (1 Peter 1:24, 25; cf. Calvin, *Commentaries*, XXII:57–60). The promise of indefectibility is not toward a particular congregation or denomination or generation or family of churches or a passing period of history, but rather the whole church to preserve her from fundamental error in the long course of history (Matt. 28:20; *Longer Catechism of the Eastern Orthodox Church*).

This kindles the celebration of thesis four: *Insofar as the faithful are sustained by pure Word and Sacrament, adhering to the "faith once delivered," their Eucharist sacrifice, Christ's own self-giving to redeem sin, is received by God as faultless, unblemished* (Ambrose, *Six Days of Creation*, IV, 2, 7; John Chrysostom, *On Eutrophius; Confession of Dositheus*, 10–12). The church "does not err, so long as it relies upon the rock of Christ, and upon the foundation of the prophets and apostles" declared the Second Helvetic Confession. Due to the Spirit's guidance, all those called will not be allowed to err at the same time. While grace does not coerce, neither does it ever bat zero in any given ecclesiastical season. It is unthinkable that God would create the church at great cost, only to let it fall irredeemably into permanent or irremediable error.

This is further undergirded by a fifth positive thesis: *Indefectibility is more a teaching of the power of the Holy Spirit than of the self-sufficiency of human imagination or of the strategic wisdom of the church as a sociological entity.* The Holy Spirit is promised to "teach you all things and will remind you of everything I have said to you" (John 14:26). The great and reliable memory of the church is lodged in God and the Holy Spirit. Always some seed of faith remains buried in the ashes even of the most divided and corrupt church. Sometimes such seeds may seem to survive marginally as semi-endangered species, as scattered all too thinly throughout the weed-infested world as remnants of former vitalities of covenant communities. Yet wherever Word and Sacrament are being faithfully transmitted, they are never without effect for "my Word [shall] . . . not return to me empty but will accomplish what I desire" (Is. 55:11), says the Lord. Although the church in some cultures appears nearly extinct, becoming "so obscured and defaced that the Church seems almost quite razed out," as the Second Helvetic Confession maintains, "yet, in the meantime the Lord has in this world, even in this darkness, his true worshippers" (cf. 1 Kings 19:18; Rev. 7:4, 9). The foundation is standing sure, and the Lord knows who are his (2 Tim. 2:9), as we have recently rediscovered in the church in China during the Cultural Revolution and in Cuba under fading "Fidelismo" and especially post-Soviet Russian spirituality.

One year after a major political reversal in the United States and six years after the fall of the Berlin Wall, today we are unpretentiously celebrating a central ironic fact of our history, which suggests a sixth thesis for active inquiry: *Classic Christians have healthily survived the death of modernity and joyfully flourish in this post-modern environment.* To all sufferers from decadent modernity, I bring greetings on behalf of the young classicists of the post-liberal underground that abides patiently in the crevices of our heartsick modern culture. They bear good news to harassed Christian believers who may be tempted to despair over the momentum of these times. They are providing walking/talking reasons why despair is a less appropriate response to these times than responsibility-taking gratitude for the grace which calls us to repentance. Against all predictions of the once confident secularizers, disciplined Christian spirituality is still vitally flourishing. I speak of the impassioned values of an emerging group of young, orthodox, cultural renovators who, having understood the values and methods of modern inquiry, and having been disillusioned by their consequences, are now turning in earnest to classical Christianity. They are young in spirit because they are not intimidated by modernity or its aftermath.

I call them "young fogeys" to distinguish them as post-modern pacesetters from the "old fogeys" who remain bogged down in the quagmire of an older liberal pietism. The young fogeys are those who are discovering the ancient Christian exegeses of the first five centuries as the deeper basis for the critique of modern pretenses to moral superiority. Their seasoned critique turns out to be more discerning than the trendier re-imaginings. Anyone who has discovered the power of that critique is a young fogey.

The young fogeys are grass-rooted, risk-capable, street smart, populist, pragmatic renovators of the apostolic tradition. They are mostly recent graduates of excellent universities, yet tough-minded critics of the ideological tilt of those institutions. They understand that the surest form of cultural renovation begins one by one with personal religious conversion, the turning of the heart away from arrogance and folly and toward faith in God. They are the newest work of the Holy Spirit.

My own generation of liberated theologians were novelty-fixated sixties revolutionaries. We applied our radical chic imagination to everything that seemed to us slightly old or dated. The emerging young classicists are critics of my generation's modern chauvinism. Thousands of well-argued older books have been torn out of our libraries and thrown out as a testament to our modern prejudice, that assumes that newer is better, older is worse. As I empathize with and speak for and about this spirited, emergent generation of young classic Christian men and women, I find myself entering into a kind of resistance movement in relation to my own generation of relativists, who have botched things up pretty absolutely. These young classicists are patient post-critical moles who persist resolutely in the cracks of the shaking foundations of the waning modern culture. They await their innings in the batting order of historical succession. These are post-modern paleo-orthodox young mentors, pastors, and professors. My young friends are sitting by the bedside of morose old-line establishments that have a gloomy prognosis, but within which a vital remnant remains. The best of them know that time is on their side, and, so far as time goes, God has plenty of it.

This leads to the seventh noteworthy thesis: *The textual core of the mainline churches' doctrine is unexpectedly secure, and formally holding fast, even when functionally ignored.* In my own sometimes prodigal communion, for example, the young fogeys take special comfort that we have been given an unyielding constitutional tradition in which there is written indelibly into church law a restriction on what legislative bodies can do. It is analogous to the Bill of Rights, and it is what Methodists call the "First Restrictive Rule," that the General Conference does not have the power under the constitution to amend, revise or otherwise tinker with the Twenty-Five Articles of Religion and the traditional classicist doctrinal standards of our church tradition. Hence in the erratic, mercurial, unpredictable doctrinal winds of culturally accommodative, ideologically chic liberal Protestantism, this classic, constitutional, doctrinal center remains defiantly intact and unchallengable. It galls the neo-pagan feminists and permissive amoralists and quasi-Marxist liberators and justification-by-equality syncretists that they cannot change that Restrictive Rule.

We can now speak confidently of the appearance of postmodern classic Christian spirituality, an emergent form of classic Christian discipline which is being born amid the demise of modernity. This requires an eighth thesis to define the modern condition: *By "modernity," we mean the period, the ideology, and the malaise of the time from 1789 to 1989, from the Bastille to the Berlin Wall; by "post-modern," we mean the course of actual history following the death of modernity; and by "classic Christian," we point to all who live faithfully out of the confession of the Apostles' Creed.* The reappropriation of classic Christian discipline is not a sentimental return to pre-modern methods or cosmology or psychology, as if the achievements of modernity were to be circumvented; rather, it is a rigorous, painstaking rebuilding from the crash of modernity using treasures old and new for moral and spiritual reconstruction. Youthful classic Christians have been rigorously prepared by modernity to use the methods of modernity (scientific, historical, hermeneutical, psychological, sociological and behavioral change models) to detoxify the illusions of modernity that have eaten like acids into the bone of the hypertolerationist church. Writers like Lewis and Chesterton—who have resisted the illusions of modernity—I do not consider to be quintessentially modern, but rather anticipated post-modernism, since they were grounded in pre-modern wisdoms.

This requires a ninth forthright hypothesis: *The leading axiom of post-modern Christian spirituality is not that modernity is corrupt, but that it is obsolete, passé, antiquated.* Hence post-modern Christian spirituality is not accurately defined as anti-modern, for there is no reason to be opposed to something that is morose. A frustrated anti-modern emotive reaction errs in overestimating the staying power of continuing terminal modernity. What makes this Christian consciousness "post" is the fact that it is no longer intimidated by the increasingly vulnerable philosophical and moral assumptions of modernity. Many in the liberal Protestant intellectual leadership have doubly paid their dues to modernity and now search for forgotten wisdoms long ruled out by the narrowly fixated dogmas of enlightenment empiricism and idealism. There is no way for us to reflect upon modernity except amid the collapse of modernity. Yet there is no time for classic Christian consciousness, under the instruction of Athanasius, Augustine, and Calvin, to despair over modernity. There is no reason to fight something already dead from the neck down. So the post-modern paleo-orthodox do not consider themselves anti-modern. They celebrate the providence of God that works amid the world that must suffer and live amidst the wreckage strewn in the pathway of modern ideologies.

We are at the end of the naive Protestant old-line which has identified so closely with modernity. We have come to the last stop on the old line, with its defensive, self-righteous elitism which hides the call to repentance and faith in God. But, as we see in thesis ten: *The end of the old line is the ironic beginning of a new line, a reversal of trajectory, a new era for disciplined classic Christian spirituality.* We are now being freed to ask what the Spirit is calling us to ponder and do to renew the historic vitalities of classic Christian spiritual formation and community building. What staple forms of Christian teaching and spirituality are most transformative amid the present cultural crisis? Can grass-roots local communities of faith lead the general church toward bottom-up renewal? Are we moving towards readiness to set realistic objectives confidently shared by moderates and traditionalists, by evangelicals and Catholics, for a reclaiming of classic Christian teaching within this ebbing millennium? What options are proffered by grace as possible remedies: petitionary?, declaratory?, legislative?, pedagogical? That is what we must debate.

Underlying this debate, is the background premise which forms an eleventh auspicious thesis: *There is an emerging resolve in the worldwide family of Protestant churches to renew the classic spiritual disciplines that have characterized the apostolic faith in all ages.* And here I speak of what all Orthodox, Catholic, Lutheran, Reformed, Anglican, Wesleyan and free church connections of spiritual formation have heard a thousand times: (1) on daily meditative study of the written Word under the guidance of the Spirit; (2) on an earnest life of personal prayer—a daily order of praise, confession, pardon, and petition for grace and using of the means of grace in common worship; (3) on mutual care of souls with intensive primary group accountability; (4) on an ordering of daily vocational life in which persons seek faithfully to walk by grace in the way of holiness—regardless of how the world interprets it; and (5) on complete yielding of the mind, heart, and will to the glory of God.

This suggests a modest twelfth thesis: *Having been disillusioned by the illusions of modernity, young post-modern Christians are now engaged in a low-key, quiet, determined effort to return to the spiritual disciplines that not only have profoundly shaped our history and common life but have in fact enabled our survival of modernity.* This emergent consciousness remains small in scale and modest in influence, and is still being chiefly advocated by those whom Wesley called "young, unknown, inconsiderable men" (*Scriptural Christianity,* iv. 11) and women. Post-modern classic Christian spirituality should not be exaggerated as if it were a politically viable movement or a world-historical spectacle that might appear unexpectedly on the cover of next week's *Time* or *Newsweek.* But it nonetheless is an observable event: the reappearance of determined, ardent, classic Christian doctrine and discipline in a post-Freudian, post-socialistic, post-quantum physics, post-Holocaust, post-modern world.

This intertwines with the thirteenth thesis: *Post-modernity in this paleo-Orthodox definition is simply that historical information that necessarily must follow the era of spent modernity, the time span from 1789 to 1989 that characteristically embraced an Enlightenment worldview that cast an ideological spell over our times and is now fading from the scene.* The fading phase of late modernity is epitomized by the reductive naturalism of Freud that is no longer marketable as an effective therapy, the idealistic historical utopianism of Marx that is now in collapse from St. Petersburg to Havana, the narcissistic assertiveness of Nietzsche which is drastically cutting life expectancy on Miami streets, and the modern chauvinism typified by Feuerbach, Dewey, and Bultmann that imagines the ethos of late modernity to be the unquestioned cultural norm that presumes to judge all premodern texts and ideas. Under that norm, sex has been reduced to orgasm, persons to bodies, psychology to stimuli, economics to planning mechanisms, politics to machinery, and the spirit to appetite. But this norm and the ideologies that spawned it are today everywhere in crisis, even while still being fawned over by liberal church bureaucratic elites.

Those evangelically-founded and once-funded institutions, bureaucracies, boards, agencies, universities and seminaries that have most lusted to adapt snugly to terminal modernity now remain behind the curve, following the wave, and not up to speed with the actual reversals of contemporary history. A fourteenth thesis now begs to be unpacked: *The liberal old-line Protestant knowledge elites (especially the media gatekeepers, Machiavellian pedagogues, and quixotic bureaucrats) are slow in grasping the moral sensibilities that have long since been grasped by those being more intentionally reformed by classic Christian spiritual disciplines.* Even if these dated modern habituations, fornicating hedonisms, me-first individualisms, reductive naturalisms, and self-destructive nihilisms may seem to have hegemony in some church bureaucracies and church-related forms of the academy, scratch the surface, and you will recognize their extreme precariousness and defensiveness. The heart is gone from the idyllic song of inevitable progress. It has become a dirge with a "heavy metal" beat.

These tired modern illusions are woven together in an ideological temperament that still sentimentally shapes the knowledge elite of the liberal Protestant ethos, especially its politicized bureaucracies, spin doctors, and academics, who remain largely unprepared to grasp either their own vulnerability, or the divine requirement, or their own possibility within this decisive situation of historical reversal. The Marxism-Leninism of the Soviet era is now gone; the Freudian idealization of sexual liberation has found it easier to make babies than parent them morally; the children of the post-psychoanalytic culture are at peril; the truculence of Nietzschean nihilism has spread to the bloody banks of Cambodian rivers with a trail of genocide along the way; the modern chauvinism of once-confident old Bultmannians is now moribund, since the enduring modernity we expected never arrived. Hence an often overlooked fifteenth thesis: *These once-assured ideologies are now unmasked as having a dated vision of the human possibility; for none have succeeded in transmitting an intergenerational culture.* Since each has colluded to support the other, they are now falling synchronously like huge ivory tower dominoes: the command economies, the backfiring therapeutic experiments, the patient-abusing therapists, the mythic fantasies of "demythology," the interpersonal fragments and splinters of narcissism, and their wholly owned ecclesiastical subsidiaries, theological hirelings and flunkies. If the Freudian project, the Bultmannian project, the Marxist project, and the Nietzschean project are all functionally moribund, then late modernity is dead. That is what is meant by the phrase "terminal modernity."

Although renewing Christian classicists tarry wistfully at the frazzled end of modernity, there is no cause for demoralization, panic, or immobilized frustration. We are being invited by providence to remain open precisely to these emergent historical conditions. Even seeming retrogressions offer gracious possibilities, as was the case in the Babylonian captivity and in the case of the martyrs. This dissolution is a providential judgment of sin and a grace-laden opportunity for listening to God. Thus thesis sixteen: *Those well-instructed in classic Christian spiritual formation are prepared to understand that amid any cultural death, gracious gifts of providential guidance are being offered, and unsullied forms of providential hedging of sin in history are emerging so as to curb human folly.*

The anxieties of renewing Christians are constantly being mitigated and calmed by the premise that the Holy Spirit has promised to continue enabling the liveliness of the body of Christ. Only on the falsely-hypothesized premise of the utter default of the Holy Spirit could the called-out people come to nothing. This is the least likely premise in the Christian understanding of history. Those who willingly enslave themselves to passing idolatries should not be surprised when alluring gods are found to have clay feet. When beloved modern arrangements and systems die, the idolaters understandably grieve and feel angry and frustrated. Meanwhile the grace-enabled community can celebrate the passage through and beyond modernity and the intricate providences of history whereby each dying historical information is giving birth to new forms and refreshing occasions for living responsibly in relation to grace.

The old line that has attached itself to dying modernity is expiring as modernity expires. Thesis seventeen is: *The church that weds itself to modernity is already a widow.* The sexual experimenters, compulsive planners of others' lives, canonical text disfigurers and ultra-feminists (as distinguished from the great company of godly Christian women who are found at many different points along the scale of feminist thinking) think of themselves as "liberated," i.e., freed from oppressive, traditional constraints of all imaginable sorts, yet they are unaware of their debt to pre-modern wisdoms. Characteristically, they are doctrinally imaginative, liturgically experimental, disciplinarily non-judgmental, politically correct, morally broadminded, ethically flexible, sexually lenient, permissive, and uninhibited. In other words, they are liberated only from the classic Christian past, the patriarchalism of Christian Scriptures, and the Jewish and Christian traditions. As a former zealous liberator, I know from experience how mesmerizing this enchantment can be.

This requires an eighteenth thesis: *When the liberated have virtually no immune system against heresy, no defense whatever against perfidious teaching, no criteria for testing the legitimacy of counterfeit theological currency, it is time for the laity to reenter the arena of church reform and theological education.* Lay members of the church must grasp that they have a decisive interest in the quality and apostolicity of the ministries they have been asked to trust. Trustees of church-related educational institutions are increasingly demanding the right to know why the clergy has been so prone to political indiscretions, sexual escapades, and ideological binges.

Innocents who do not know the arcane internal machinery of theological education have no reason to doubt that the seminary, like any other institution, is easily reformable. But those who have spent a lifetime in increasingly tradition-starved theological settings are those most convinced that the present system is practically unreformable. The tenured, iconoclastic faculty is so intractable that, lacking a special act of grace, reform is virtually unimaginable. This requires another thesis, number nineteen: *The tenure principle which was designed to protect academic and spiritual freedom has become so exploited in some settings as now to protect academic and spiritual license, absenteeism, incompetence, and at times moral turpitude, since once tenure is offered, it is virtually impossible to withdraw.* If the "liberated" have the freedom to teach apostasy, the believing church has the freedom to withhold its consent. If they teach counter-canonical doctrines and conjectures inimical to the health of the church, the church has no indelible moral obligation to give them support or bless their follies.

Thus we come sadly to our most dismal thesis, number twenty: *Once a tradition-retrogressive leadership has been filled with permanently-tenured radicals, its members are given the unique privilege of cloning themselves with look-alike future colleagues.* Can those shaped by the classic Christian spiritual disciplines remain in good conscience in an ecclesiastical system that has gone so far afield? The major reason for staying the course is that if they leave, the patient is left in the hands of the euthanasia advocates, the Kervorkians of the liberal old line. The vocational dilemma for the young fogeys is this: If they stay in, they may be co-opted, since they must work within a nearly totally corrupt and corrupting system. But walking away turns out to have much weightier moral impediments than staying to do battle. The young fogeys are refusing to vacate the premises, concede defeat, and capitulate to inevitability because of thesis twenty-one: *It is unthinkable to abandon, without further prayers for special grace, an institution to which so many of the faithful have committed themselves and have supported with their personal and often scarce resources over so long a time.*

But can the liberated ecclesiastical elites be significantly reshaped? Not without an basic reversal of abuses that promote ideological cloning in education for ministry. Hence thesis twenty-two: *There is no way to continue the present tenure system and reform the tradition-impaired theological seminary.* A clean sweep seems at once impossible and necessary. There is a profound need for prayer for special grace, and indeed for an army of intercession for the reform of theological education. A strongly organized and involved laity, and determined trustees are also needed.

My twenty-third thesis is this: *The real moral embarrassment of the rhetoric of 'inclusivism' is its lack of honest inclusiveness, its willful exclusion of non-liberals, and those who resist absolute relativism.* Classic Christians must learn how to communicate to liberal colleagues how hollow the inclusion arguments sound to traditional believers who themselves are being marginalized and persecuted. This is our opportunity to put to work the oppression analysis that the liberated church has espoused, turning it back upon its primary users and abusers.

Thesis twenty-four follows: *When avant garde academics bandy about the term "postmodern," the wary do well to strike "post" and insert "ultra."* For guild scholars, the term "post-modern" typically means simply modern to the nth degree. The waning value assumptions of modernity are nostalgically recollected, and ancient wisdoms are compulsively disregarded. Meanwhile, the real post-modernism that is happening outside the liberals' ivory towers is not yet recognized or understood. Card-carrying ultra-moderns may talk a fine game of post-modernity, but it is time for those who have patiently sat through repetitive exercises in liberal guilt to assert the truth about their illsions. They lack true "peer review" because they do not associate with colleagues who hold views different from their own.

What is now clear is that a once dominant liberal world-view is ebbing. It is not wholly extinct yet, but it is numb and lacks vitality. Autonomous individualism, narcissistic hedonism, reductive naturalism, and absolute moral relativism are dying, and they are the heartbeat of terminal modernity. What is happening amid this historical situation is a joyous return to the sacred texts of Christian Scripture. This leads to a summarizing, final thesis, which is indeed heartening: *The young fogeys, the surviving paleo-orthodox, are those who—having entered in good faith into the disciplines of modernity and having become disillusioned with its illusions—are again studying the texts of the ancient Christian tradition which point to the Word of God revealed in history as attested by prophetic and apostolic witnesses whose testimonies have become perennial authoritative Scripture for this worldwide, multicultural, multigenerational remembering and celebrating community.*

What If Jesus Had Never Been Born?*

D. James Kennedy
(with Jerry Newcombe)

D. James Kennedy is the most listened to Presbyterian minister in the world today. His television and radio broadcasts are heard in 25,000 cities and towns across America. He heads up five major ministries. He is the senior minister of the Coral Ridge Presbyterian Church, which has over 8,000 members and has been cited by *Decision* magazine as one of the top five churches in the nation. He is the president of Evangelism Explosion International, which trains laymen in evangelism in 190 countries and 300 denominations. He also oversees the Westminster Academy, a K-12 school for over 1,000 students, and is chancellor of Knox Theological Seminary. Finally, he is president of Coral Ridge Ministries, a national network television ministry that was launched in 1978. Its one-hour telecast is broadcast on more than 470 stations and five cable networks and is also broadcast overseas. Its radio program is regularly heard on over 500 stations.

We live in an age in which only one prejudice is tolerated—anti-Christian bigotry. Michael Novak, the eminent religious writer, once said that today you can no longer hold up to public pillorying and ridicule groups such as African-Americans or Native Americans or women or homosexuals or Poles, and so on. Today, the only group you can hold up to public mockery is Christians. Attacks on the Church and Christianity are common. As Pat Buchanan once put it, "Christian-bashing is a popular indoor sport."

But the truth is this: Had Jesus never been born, this world would be far more miserable than it is. In fact, many of man's noblest and kindest deeds find their motivation in love for

*Excerpted from *What If Jesus Had Never Been Born* (Nashville: Thomas Nelson Publishers, 1994).

143

Jesus Christ; and some of our greatest accomplishments also have their origin in service rendered to the humble Carpenter of Nazareth.

A Quick Overview of Christ's Impact on World History

Some people have made transformational changes in one department of human learning or in one aspect of human life, and their names are forever enshrined in the annals of human history. But Jesus Christ, the greatest man who ever lived, has changed virtually every aspect of human life—and most people don't know it. The greatest tragedy of the Christmas holiday each year is not so much its commercialization, but its trivialization. How tragic it is that people have forgotten Him to whom they owe so very much.

Everything that Jesus Christ touched, He utterly transformed. He touched time when He was born into this world; He had a birthday and that birthday utterly altered the way we measure time.[1] Someone has said, "He has turned aside the river of ages out of its course and lifted the centuries off their hinges." Now, the whole world counts time as Before Christ (B.C.) and A.D. Unfortunately, in most cases, our illiterate generation today doesn't even know that A.D. means *Anno Domini,* "In the year of the Lord."

The Growth of the Mustard Seed

Jesus said that the kingdom of heaven is like a mustard seed, which is tiny in and of itself; but, when fully grown, it provides shade and a resting place for many birds. This parable certainly applies to an individual who embraces Christ; it also applies to Christianity in the world.

Christianity's roots were small and humble—an itinerant rabbi preached and did miracles for three and a half years around the countryside of subjugated Israel. And today there are more than 1.8 billion professing believers in Him found in most of the nations on earth![2] There are tens of millions today who make it their life's aim to serve Him alone. Emperors and governors were the men with power in Christ's day.

But now their bodies rot in their sepulchres, and their souls await the Final Judgment. They have no followers today. No one worships them. No one serves them or awaits their bidding.

Not so with Jesus! Napoleon, who was well accustomed to political power, said that it would be amazing if a Roman emperor could rule from the grave, and yet that is what Jesus has been doing. (We would disagree with him, though, in that Jesus is not dead; He's alive.) Napoleon said: "I search in vain in history to find the similar to Jesus Christ, or anything which can approach the gospel... nations pass away, thrones crumble, but the Church remains."[3] A brief, anonymous composition of the nineteenth century also puts Christ's life and influence into perspective:

> He was born in an obscure village, the child of a peasant woman. He grew up in another village, where He worked in a carpenter shop until He was thirty. Then for three years He was an itinerant preacher. He never wrote a book. He never held an office. He never had a family or owned a home. He didn't go to college. He never visited a big city. He never traveled two hundred miles from the place where He was born. He did none of the things that usually accompany greatness. He had no credentials but Himself.

> He was only thirty-three when the tide of public opinion turned against Him. His friends ran away. One of them denied Him. He was turned over to His enemies and went through the mockery of a trial. He was nailed to a cross between two thieves.

> While He was dying, His executioners gambled for His garments, the only property He had on earth. When He was dead, He was laid in a borrowed grave through the pity of a friend. Nineteen centuries have come and gone, and today He is the central figure of the human race.

> All the armies that ever marched, all the navies that ever sailed, all the parliaments that ever sat, all the kings that ever reigned, put together, have not affected the life of man on this earth as much as that one solitary life.

We should also remember that, despite its humble origins, the Church has made more changes on earth for the good than any other movement or force in history. To get an overview of some of the positive contributions Christianity has made through the centuries, here are a few highlights:

- Hospitals, which essentially began during the Middle Ages.
- Universities, which also began during the Middle Ages. In addition, most of the world's greatest universities were started by Christians for Christian purposes.
- Literacy and education for the masses.
- Capitalism and free-enterprise.
- Representative government, particularly as it has been seen in the American experiment.
- The separation of political powers.
- Civil liberties.
- The abolition of slavery, both in antiquity and in more modern times.
- Modern science.
- The discovery of the New World by Columbus.
- The elevation of women.
- Benevolence and charity; the good Samaritan ethic.
- Higher standards of justice.
- The elevation of the common man.
- The condemnation of adultery, homosexuality, and other sexual perversions.
- High regard for human life.
- The civilizing of many barbarian and primitive cultures.
- The codifying and setting to writing of many of the world's languages.
- Greater development of art and music. The inspiration for the greatest works of art.
- The countless lives transformed from liabilities into assets to society because of the gospel.
- The eternal salvation of countless souls!

The last one mentioned, the salvation of souls, is the primary goal of the spread of Christianity. All the other benefits listed are basically just by-products of what Christianity has often brought when applied to daily living.

When Jesus Christ took upon Himself the form of man, He imbued mankind with a dignity and inherent value that had never been dreamed of before. Whatever Jesus touched or whatever He did transformed that aspect of human life. Many people read about the innumerable small incidents in the life of Christ while never dreaming that those casually mentioned "little" things were to transform the history of humankind.

If Jesus Had Never Been Born

Many are familiar with the 1946 film classic, *It's a Wonderful Life,* wherein the character played by Jimmy Stewart gets a chance to see what life would be like had he never been born. The main point of the film is that each person's life has impact on everybody else's life. Had they never been born, there would be gaping holes left by their absence. My point here is that Jesus Christ has had enormous impact—more than anybody else—on history. Had He never come, the hole would be a canyon about the size of a continent.

Not all have been happy about Jesus Christ's coming into the world. Friedrich Nietzsche, the nineteenth-century atheist philosopher who coined the phrase "God is dead," likened Christianity to poison that has infected the whole world.[4] He said of Jesus: "He died too early; he himself would have revoked his doctrine had he reached [greater maturity]!"[5] And Nietzsche said that history is the battle between Rome (the pagans) and Israel (the Jews and the Christians);[6] and he bemoaned the fact that Israel (through Christianity) was winning and that the cross "has by now triumphed over all other, nobler virtues."[7] In his book, *The AntiChrist,* Nietzsche wrote:

> I *condemn* Christianity; I bring against the Christian Church the most terrible of all the accusations that an accuser has ever had in his mouth. It is, to me, the greatest of all imaginable corruptions; it seeks to work the ultimate corruption, the worst possible corruption. The Christian Church has left nothing un-

touched by its depravity; it has turned every value into worthlessness, and every truth into a lie, and every integrity into baseness of soul.[8]

Nietzsche held up as heroes a "herd of blond beasts of prey, a race of conquerors and masters."[9] According to Nietzsche, and later Hitler, by whom or what were these Teutonic warriors corrupted? The answer was: Christianity. "This splendid ruling stock was corrupted, first by the Catholic laudation of feminine virtues, secondly by the Puritan and plebeian ideals of the Reformation, and thirdly by intermarriage with inferior stock."[10] Had Jesus never come, wailed Nietzsche, we would never have had the corruption of "slave morals" into the human race. Many of the ideas of Nietzsche were put into practice by his philosophical disciple, Hitler, and about 16 million people died as a result.[11]

In *Mein Kampf,* Hitler blamed the Church for perpetuating the ideas and laws of the Jews. Hitler wanted to completely uproot Christianity once he had finished uprooting the Jews. In a private conversation "shortly after the National Socialists' rise to power,"[12] recorded by Herman Rauschning, Hitler said:

> Historically speaking, the Christian religion is nothing but a Jewish sect. . . . After the destruction of Judaism, the extinction of Christian slave morals must follow logically. . . . I shall know the moment when to confront, for the sake of the German people and the world, their Asiatic slave morals with our picture of the free man, the godlike man. . . . It is not merely a question of Christianity and Judaism. We are fighting against the most ancient curse that humanity has brought upon itself. We are fighting against the perversion of our soundest instincts. Ah, the God of the deserts, that crazed, stupid, vengeful Asiatic despot with his powers to make laws! . . . That poison with which both Jews and Christians have spoiled and soiled the free, wonderful instincts of man and lowered them to the level of doglike fright.[13]

Both Nietzsche and Hitler wished that Christ had never been born. Others share this sentiment. For example, Charles Lam Markmann, who wrote a favorable book on the history of the ACLU, entitled *The Noblest Cry,* has said: "If the otherwise admirably civilized pagans of Greece and their Roman successors had had the wit to laugh Judaism into desuetude, the world would have been spared the 2000-year sickness of Christendom."[14]

Interestingly, people living under Nazi oppression, under Stalin's terror, under Mao's cultural revolution, and the reign of the Khmer Rouge were all spared "the 2000-year sickness of Christendom"! Contrary to Markmann's armchair philosophizing, civil liberties have been bequeathed by Christianity and not by atheism or humanism.

Stalin and Mao both tried to destroy Christianity in their respective domains.[15] In the process, they slaughtered tens of millions of professing Christians, but they utterly failed in their ultimate objective. Christianity survives, and it continues to make important contributions to world civilization. Of course, there are negative aspects of the Church's track record in history. We should always deal forthrightly with the sins of the Church, and we should come to grips—from a Christian perspective—with such blots on the past as the Crusades, the Inquisition, and anti-Semitism. But we must never lose sight of the danger of abandoning our faith. The post-Christian West ventured into a much more bloody history in the 20th century precisely because so many of the restraints of traditional Christianity were removed.

Christianity's Impact on the Value of Human Life

"What is the most important thing to come out of a mine?" asked a French engineer of his students about a century ago. After the pupils named various minerals, he corrected them: "The most important thing to come out of the mine was the miner."[16] I agree and submit that this view of human life is embraced only where the gospel of Jesus Christ has deeply penetrated. Prior to the coming of Christ, human life on this planet was exceedingly cheap. Life was expendable prior to Christianity's influence. Even today, in parts of the world where the gospel of Christ or Christianity has not penetrated, life is exceedingly cheap. But Jesus Christ—He who said, "Behold, I make all things new" (Rev. 21:5)—gave mankind a new perspective on the value of human life. Furthermore, Christianity bridged the gap between the Jews—who first received the divine revelation that man was made in God's image—and the pagans, who attributed little value to human life. Meanwhile, as we in the post-Christian West abandon our Judeo-Christian heritage, life is becoming cheap once again.

Children

In the ancient world, child sacrifice was a common phenomenon. Archaeologists have unearthed ancient cemeteries, near pagan temples, of babies that had been sacrificed—for example, in what used to be Carthage. Before the Jewish conquest of the promised land, child sacrifice among the Canaanites was commonplace. The prophets of the ancient god Baal and his wife, Ashtoreth, commonly practiced child sacrifice as part of their worship. Earlier this century, the Oriental Institute of the University of Chicago did some excavating in Samaria in "the stratum of Ahab's time,"[17] digging up ruins of a temple of Ashtoreth. Halley states:

> Just a few steps from this temple was a cemetery, where many jars were found, containing remains of infants who had been sacrificed in this temple.... Prophets of Baal and Ashtoreth were official murderers of little children. But it wasn't just in the Near East that the value of human life was in low esteem.[18]

That's because life was cheap all over, in the Near East, in the Middle East, in the Far East.

It was a dangerous thing for a baby to be conceived in classical Rome or Greece, just as it is becoming dangerous once more under the influence of the modern pagan. In those days abortion was rampant. Abandonment was commonplace: It was usual for infirm babies or unwanted little ones to be taken out into the forest or the mountainside, to be consumed by wild animals or to starve or to be picked up by rather strange people who crept around at night, and then would use them for whatever perverted purposes they had in mind. Parents abandoned virtually all deformed babies. Many parents abandoned babies if they were poor. They often abandoned female babies because women were considered inferior.

To make matters worse, those children who outlived infancy—approximately two-thirds of those born[19]—were the property of their father; he could kill them at his whim. Only about half of the children born lived beyond the age of eight,[20] in part because of widespread infanticide, with famine and disease also being contributing factors. Infanticide was not only legal; it was applauded. Killing a Roman was murder, but it was commonly held in Rome that killing one's own children could be an act of beauty. The father exercised an absolute tyranny over his children. He could kill them; he could sell them as slaves; he could marry them off; he could divorce them; he could confiscate their property.

In his book *Third Time Around*—telling how the Church has twice successfully fought abortion in the past and how today the Church is once again on the forefront in the fight against abortion—George Grant adds further insight into just how valueless human life was in ancient Rome:

> According to the centuries old tradition of *paterfamilias*, the birth of a Roman was not a biological fact. Infants were received into the world only as the family willed. A Roman did not *have* a child; he *took* a child. Immediately after birthing, if the family decided not to *raise* the child—literally, lifting him above the earth—he was simply abandoned. There were special high places or walls where the newborn was taken and exposed to die.[21]

Robin Lane Fox, a fellow of New College, Oxford, points out how common and widespread these practices were in ancient Rome:

> Exposure was only one of several checks on reproduction. Abortion was freely practiced, and the medical sources distinguish precoital attempts at "contraception." The line, however, between the two practices was often obscure, not least in the case of drugs which were taken to "stop" unwanted children. Limitation of births was not confined to the poorer classes. Partible inheritance was universal, and as the raising of several children fragmented a rich man's assets, the number of his heirs was often curbed deliberately. As men of all ages slept with their slaves, natural children were a widespread fact of life. However, they followed the servile status of their mother, while laws of

inheritance and social status did discriminate against any who were born from free parents.[22]

In short, it was dangerous to be conceived and born in the ancient world. Human life was exceedingly cheap.

But then Jesus came. He did not disdain to be conceived in the virgin's womb, but He humbled Himself to be found in fashion as a man. Since that time, Christians have cherished life as sacred, even the life of the unborn. In ancient Rome, Christians saved many of these babies and brought them up in the faith. Similarly, this very day, despite a virtual media blackout, Christians are helping thousands of pregnant women through the 3,000 pro-life crisis pregnancy centers around the country.[23]

Abortion disappeared in the early Church. Infanticide and abandonment disappeared. The cry went out to bring the children to Church. Foundling homes, orphanages, and nursery homes were started to house the children. These new practices, based on this higher view of life, helped to create a foundation in Western civilization for an ethic of human life that persists to this day—although it is currently under severe attack. And it all goes back to Jesus Christ. If He had never been born, we would never have seen this change in the value of human life.

A dismal fate awaited the youngsters of ancient Rome, Greece, India, and China. Herod slaughtered the innocents, but the advent of Christ was the triumph of the innocents. Jesus gathered the little children unto Himself saying, "Let the little children come to Me, and do not forbid them" (Matt. 19:14a). His words gave a new importance to children, an importance that bestowed dignified treatment upon them. After Jesus said that God was our Father, not only did this radically alter the attitudes of fathers toward children, but fatherhood in this life asssumed a completely new form as well.

Through His Church, ultimately Jesus brought an end to infanticide. The influence of Christ brought value to human life, and infanticide was outlawed. It lost favor with Christians who viewed it as an outrageous crime. Christian influence in the Roman Empire helped to enshrine in law Christian principles of the sacredness of human life. More than twenty years ago, Sherwood Wirt, at the time the editor of Billy Graham's *Decision* magazine, wrote an important book called *The Social Conscience of the Evangelical*. Wirt points out the positive influences for human life that the Church of Jesus Christ was able to effect, for example, through emperors who were professing Christians:

> Many permanent legal reforms were set in motion by Emperors Constantine (280?-337) and Justinian (483–565) that can be laid to the influence of Christianity. Licentious and cruel sports were checked; new legislation was ordered to protect the slave, the prisoner, the mutilated man, the outcast woman. Children were granted important legal rights. Infant exposure was abolished. Women were raised from a status of degradation to that of legal protection. Hospitals and orphanages were created to take care of foundlings. Personal feuds and private wars were put under restraint. . . . Branding of slaves was halted.[24]

Wirt quotes a second-century "Letter to Diognetus," wherein the writer states that Christians "marry . . . they beget children; but they do not destroy their offspring."[25] The implication in this statement is that child killing was common at the time, except among Christians.

The role of the sixth-century Christian Emperor Justinian on behalf of human life is profound. Put in simplistic terms, Justinian had his top jurists compile what they believed to be the best of previous codes of law and judicial opinions into one summary, which—along with a few of Justinian's own edicts—is now known as "the Justinian Code." The Justinian code was explicit in declaring infanticide and abortion illegal:

> Those who expose children, possibly hoping they would die, and those who use the potions of the abortionist, are subject to the full penalty of the law—both civil and ecclesiastical—for murder. Should exposure occur, the finder of the child is to see that he is baptized and that he is treated with Christian care and compassion. They may be then adopted as *ad scriptitiorum*— even as we ourselves have been adopted into the kingdom of grace.[26]

George Grant points out that in the seventh century, the Council of Vaison met to "reiterate and expand that pro-life mandate by encouraging the faithful to care for the unwanted and to give relief to the distressed."[27] At that time, the Church reaffirmed its commitment to adoption as the alternative to abortion.

Grant demonstrates how, in centuries past, the Church—through word and deed—gave rise to a pro-life view of humanity. After reviewing much of the evidence for how the early Church and the medieval Church impacted the value of human life, Grant sums up:

> Before the explosive and penetrating growth of medieval Christian influence, the primordial evils of abortion, infanticide, abandonment, and exposure were a normal part of everyday life in Europe. Afterward, they were regarded as the grotesque perversions that they actually are. That remarkable new pro-life consensus was detonated by a cultural reformation of cosmic proportions. It was catalyzed by civil decrees, ecclesiastical canons, and merciful activity. . . . Assaults on the bastion of that great medieval legacy have been fierce and furious during the five-hundred-odd years since the fall of Constantinople and the passing of the medieval mantle. But battered and bedraggled as it is, it still stands—vivid testimony to the depth of its foundation.[28]

Today we take many of these ideas for granted in the West because they have been so embedded in our culture for centuries. But had Christ never been born, it would have been a far different story—human life would be quite cheap!

Women

Prior to Christian influence, a woman's life was also very cheap. In ancient cultures, the wife was the property of her husband. In India, China, Rome, and Greece, people felt and declared that women were not able or competent to be independent (although in Rome, particularly in the third century, some women of the upper class were asserting themselves). Aristotle said that a woman was somewhere between a free man and a slave. When we understand how valueless a slave was in ancient times, we get a glimpse of how bad a woman's fate was back then. Plato taught that if a man lived a cowardly life, he would be reincarnated as a woman. If she lived a cowardly life, she would be reincarnated as a bird.

In ancient Rome we find that a woman's lot was not much better—for those who survived infancy. Little girls were abandoned in far greater numbers than boys. In *Pagans and Christians,* Robin Lane Fox points out that the killing of infant girls was so widespread it affected marriage customs:

> In antiquity, this pattern [the postponement of marriage] is not so evident, because of *the widespread habit of exposing female babies at birth.* Adult girls were in shorter supply and thus their age at marriage tended to be low. . . . Habitual exposure of babies was a further brake on the size of a family and the balance of the sexes.[29]

As we've seen, over time it was Christianity that stilled the practice of child killing, until its recent revival by the modern pagan in the practice of abortion.

The killing of baby girls simply because of their sex was not only a practice in the ancient world. When missionaries or European explorers came into contact with foreign lands that had not been affected by the gospel, they found similar appalling practices—with baby girls, in particular, being the targets. For example, two Norwegian women missionaries in the last century—Sofie Reuter and Anna Jakobsen—found infanticide of little girls a common practice in late nineteenth-century China. Writing in 1880, they declared:

> It is an exception that a couple would have more than one or two girls. If there would be more born, they would be disposed of immediately. It was done in different ways. She could simply be put out as food for wild dogs and wolves. The father would sometimes take her to a "baby tower," where she would soon die of exposure and starvation and be discovered by birds of prey. Others again would bury the little ones under the dirt floor in the room where they were born . If there is a river flowing by, the children would be thrown in it.[30]

Adam Smith, writing in 1776, confirms this in his book *The Wealth of Nations.* He states: "In all great towns [of China] several [babies] are every night exposed in the street, or drowned like puppies in the water. The performance of this horrid office is even said to be the avowed business by which some people earn their subsistence."[31] This was just two hundred years ago, and it was before any influence of Jesus Christ was to penetrate China.

However, in the last two centuries, because of the modern missionary movement, the lives of women have been greatly improved in scores of countries and hundreds of tribes as the gospel took root in those cultures. Take the two courageous missionaries mentioned above as an example. Reuter and Jakobsen would daily comb the abandonment places to save Chinese girls from sure death. They would then rear these girls and teach them the Christian faith.

India is another example. Prior to Christian influences in India, widows were voluntarily or involuntarily burned on their husbands' funeral pyres—a grisly practice known as *suttee*. The word itself literally translates "good woman," implying that the Hindus believed it was a good woman who followed her husband into death. As can be imagined, this practice shocked the Christian missionaries coming from the West.

Furthermore, infanticide—particularly for girls—was common in India, prior to the great missionary William Carey. Carey and other Christians detested seeing these little ones being tossed into the sea. These centuries-old practices, *suttee* and infanticide, were finally stopped only in the early nineteenth century and only through missionary agitation to the British authorities. Tragically, as Christian influence is now felt less and less in modern India, we have seen the rise of sex-selective abortions[32]—killing unborn girls—practiced widely there and indeed all over the Far East.[33]

India also had "child widows," young girls who grew up to be temple prostitutes. In the twentieth century, Amy Carmichael, a missionary of the Dohnavur Fellowship, fought this practice by weaning many girls out of this situation and into a Christian community. In the last century, Charles Spurgeon told of a Hindu woman who said to a missionary: "Surely your Bible was written by a woman." "Why?" he asked. "Because it says so many kind things about women. Our pundits never refer to us but in reproach."[34]

Prior to Christian influence, Africa had a practice similar to *sutee*. The wives and concubines of the chieftain were killed at his death. Such tribal customs were stopped after Christianity began to penetrate the continent.

In other areas of the globe where the gospel of Christ has not penetrated, the value of women's lives is cheap. Even in my lifetime, I saw in the Middle East four men playing checkers, while another man, presumably of a lower class, was plowing a field with two animals yoked to each other. One animal was an ox, but I couldn't tell what the other animal was until they turned the corner, and I saw that it was a woman! She was probably the wife of one of the men playing checkers on the porch. And I realized in what low esteem and how cheaply the lives of women were held prior to the coming of Christ. Christ did an incredible thing for women, lifting them to a high level—higher than they had ever been before.

How ironic that feminists today do not give any credit to Christ or Christianity; in fact, they say it has oppressed women. In reality, Christianity has elevated women enormously. Had Jesus never come, Gloria Steinem, had she survived childhood, would most likely be wearing a veil today!

The Elderly

It has often been said that the Chinese and Japanese worship their elders, but only after exposure to Christianity were homes built for them. Throughout history, many tribes and peoples killed off their elderly, much as they have killed off their unwanted babies. The Eskimos used to kill their elderly by setting them adrift in ice floes floating out to sea! Whatever the method, the pattern is the same. Prior to Christ, the value of the elderly was determined by the particular custom of each tribe. With Christ, *all* human life has value, including that of the elderly.

Of course, it should be pointed out that the care of the elderly wasn't always as much of an issue as it is in modern times. Even as recently as 1892, only one in 100 people worldwide lived to be over the age of 65. Only through modern medicine do we have people living as long as they do today. So this wasn't as much of an issue in past times as, say, child killing.

As we have moved away from God and His principles in this country, we are reverting to a more pagan view of life. We see the move afoot to kill off the elderly—whether it's called mercy killing or euthanasia. Some today are advocating that those elderly persons who lack a certain "quality of life" should die and get out of the way for the younger population! Today there's a hideous way of abandoning the elderly that is common enough to warrant a name: "Granny dumping." This refers to bringing an old person to a hospital or race track or some place crowded with people and abandoning him or her there.[35] We have abandoned the Judeo-Christian view of human life and substituted a tawdry one instead!

Slavery

Half of the population of the Roman Empire was enslaved. Three-fourths of the population of Athens was enslaved. The life of a slave could be taken at the whim of the master. Over the centuries, Christianity abolished slavery, first in the ancient world and then later in the nineteenth century, largely through the efforts of strong evangelicals like William Wilberforce. It didn't happen overnight, and certainly there have been dedicated Christians who were slaveowners. Nonetheless, the end of slavery, which has plagued mankind for thousands of years, has come primarily through the efforts of Christians.

The condition of the slave in the ancient world was abysmal. One scholar reminds us that in Athens it was legal to admit into a courtroom the testimony of a slave only under torture; yet the testimony of a free man was admitted under oath. Among the Romans, if the master of a household was murdered, all of his domestic slaves were put to death without legal inquiry. It was a common mark of hospitality to assign a female slave to a guest for the night, as one would any other convenience. Thus we see the crushing tyranny and degradation of the ancient, humanistic world, manifested in slavery.

This is even more disturbing when we consider that a large percentage of the population of the ancient world was made up of slaves. Wirt comments on the horrors of their condition:

> In Sparta there was systematic terrorizing of slaves. Primitive tribes around the world considered the slave to be utterly without dignity or rights. For millions upon millions of enslaved people in past centuries, and even down to the present day in outlying pockets of civilization, survival has been a matter of supreme indifference because of their condition of bondage. The warrior who preferred death to capture was not necessarily being brave or noble; he was being realistic. Even in sophisticated Athens and Rome, where household slaves received humane treatment and were accorded special privileges, their lives were never out of jeopardy. Four hundred slaves belonging to the Roman Pedanius Secundus were ordered put to death because they were under their master's roof when he was murdered.[36]

People of the same race enslaved each other in ancient times. The deities had no concern for the slaves. Slaves had no rights, no relation to society, none to the state, and none to God. But when the gospel began to take root in people's hearts, that changed over time. In that brief book of the Bible called Philemon, Paul writes from prison to Philemon, a wealthy Christian slaveowner. Paul sends the letter to Philemon with Onesimus, Philemon's runaway slave who was a fellow prisoner with Paul. Paul had led both men to Christ and in his letter tells Philemon, "Receive him (Onesimus) not as a slave, but as a brother beloved."

Millions of people in modern America have read that statement and have not been touched at all. Yet that was among the most revolutionary concepts the world had ever heard—a slave, an "animated tool," was a brother, beloved! Absolutely unthinkable and incredible! Such a simple statement, along with the concept of Christian brotherhood, melted away the fetters of slavery, like icicles before the rising sun!

Critics of Christianity like to point out that the lack of direct challenge of the institution of slavery from Paul or other leaders in the early Church constitutes a Christian complicity of sorts with slavery. In *Asimov's Guide to the Bible: The New Testament,* the late scientist and secularist Isaac Asimov wrote:

> Nevertheless, while Paul urges kindness to the slave Onesimus, who is now Philemon's brother in Christianity, there is no hint anywhere in Paul that slavery might be wrong and immoral as an institution. Indeed, Paul even admonishes slaves to obey their masters, so that Christianity, however novel some of its tenets, was by no means a doctrine of social revolution.[37]

Other secularists also make a similar point. Oxford scholar Robin Lane Fox writes that Christian leaders in the second and third centuries did nothing to disturb the institution of slavery.[38] Of the early Church, Fox observes:

> Its priorities are not those of a faith concerned to free slaves from their masters, or to urge masters to let them be released.... At most, Christian slaves were consoled and comforted.... Christian masters were not specially encouraged to set a slave free, although *Christians were most numerous in the setting of urban households where freeing was most frequent.*[39]

Fox summarizes all this by his statement: "Christians aimed to reform the heart, not the social order."[40] Both Asimov and Fox miss the big picture, however, because Christians don't assert that the Christian religion abolished slavery overnight. If Christianity totally disallowed slavery, the gospel could not have spread as it did in the early Church. Once the gospel did spread, the seeds were sown for the eventual dissolution of slavery. Thus by reforming the heart, Christianity, in time, reformed the social order. Furthermore, as Latourette points out, "Christianity undercut slavery by giving dignity to work."[41]

Alas, slavery did rear its ugly head again in more recent times at the hands of the Portuguese and the Spanish. When they discovered the black man in Africa, we had another bout with slavery. But it wasn't until men devoted their whole lives to abolishing the slave trade that action was taken. A strong 19th-century evangelical, William Wilberforce, who was a member of the British Parliament for decades, was such a man. And Wilberforce gathered other likeminded evangelicals to help him in the fight; they were known as "the Clapham Sect," since they met in Clapham, England.

The model Christian statesman in the history of the world, William Wilberforce worked tirelessly to halt the slave trade from Africa to the West Indies. After he spent twenty years diligently crusading against it, Parliament finally passed his bill to halt the slave trade. Then he worked indefatigably to free the slaves in the British territories; this battle was to last twenty-five years! Despite constant opposition and derision, he pursued his course as a service to Jesus Christ.

Wilberforce had undergone a dramatic conversion as a young man which changed his life from one of trivial pursuit to one of freeing the slaves. On his deathbed he received word that Parliament had acted and twenty million pounds had been designated to pay for the release of all remaining slaves of England. And on that day in 1833, 700,000 British slaves were freed. Wilberforce was greatly moved to know that a whole lifetime of effort on his part had finally seen fruition, and he thanked God for bringing it to pass.

Thirty years later, at far greater cost of war, after the thunderous indictments from the pulpits of the North, slavery disappeared from America. Wirt points out:

> In the Eastern and Midwestern United States the evangelicals were often drawn into the struggle against slavery. Calvinist and Methodist alike were giving spiritual support to the abolition movement in the 1840s and 1850s. The town of Oberlin, Ohio, founded by Charles G. Finney as a college for the training of evangelists, became . . . a main connecting point on the "underground railroad." President Finney himself was not above hiding fugitive slaves in his attic.[42]

We know that two-thirds of the members of the abolition society in 1835 were ministers of the gospel.[43] It is well-known that many of the leading practitioners of the Underground Railroad were Quakers. Abraham Lincoln's Christianity is well-documented; his writings are filled with Bible quotes. Ultimately, Christianity and slavery are incompatible. Robert E. Lee, who freed the slaves he had inherited by marriage, once wrote that the War between the States was needless bloodshed in terms of ending slavery, for he believed the evil institution would have eventually withered away because of Christianity.

Suicide

The sin of suicide is mentioned five times in the Bible. In over 4,000 years of biblical history, only five people took their own lives, and all five of them were wicked men, like Judas, who sold the Savior for thirty pieces of silver.

In contrast to Jewish history, many of the Roman leaders committed suicide. [44] This includes Pontius Pilate,[45] Senators Brutus and Cassius, Antony and Cleopatra (though she wasn't a Roman leader), Emperor Nero, Stoic philosopher Seneca, several gladiators in training, Emperor Hadrian, and on it goes. Historian Will Durant writes of the average Roman living by the popular Stoic philosophy, that "life itself was always to remain within his choice."[46] Thus suicide was not uncommon in ancient Rome prior to Christian influences.

Christianity has long been a foe of suicide, in the ancient world and now in the modern world. Today the neo-pagan view is cheapening the value of human life all over again. Recently, one of the nation's best-selling books was a how-to manual on suicide! But God's wisdom says, "All those who hate me love death" (Prov. 8:36).

In modern times, we have drifted from a sanctity of life ethic to a quality of life ethic. The concept of sanctity of life is a spiritual concept; it is a religious concept. The word *sanctity*—which comes from the Latin word *sanctitas* from *sanctus*—means "holy or sacred unto God, inviolable, that which God has declared is of great value." It is, therefore, a spiritual concept.

However, for a humanist or an atheist or an unbeliever of most any kind, there is no such thing as sanctity of life. Unless there is a God who has given us a spirit and who sanctifies us, there cannot be a sanctity-of-life ethic.

With such a low view of man as that introduced in the last century, should it surprise us that man has killed more of his own during the twentieth century than in all the other centuries combined? As the saying goes, "Ideas control the world." Only by the resurgence of modern paganism, in a post-Christian culture, do we find the Nazi concentration camp, the Soviet gulag, the American abortion chamber.

Quality of life is a physical concept. No one can look at another and determine the quality of that person's soul. If life is merely molecules in motion, then we can have a quality-of-life ethic. But if we are Christians and believe that there is an infinite, eternal, and unchangeable God who is Spirit, who has given us an eternal soul; and if we have an inalienable right to life, we cannot buy that kind of an ethic.

When Supreme Court Justice Harry A. Blackmun wrote *Roe* v. *Wade,* he appealed to religion. However, he said, "If I were to appeal to religion, I would appeal to the religions of Rome and Greece"—which, of course, practiced and encouraged abortion, infanticide, euthanasia, suicide. Today, many people in the Western world are reverting to heathen paganism, and most of them don't even know that it is happening.

The Value of Human Life

The morality of any society can be easily judged by the view it holds of human life. In 1844, H. L. Hastings visited the Fiji Islands. He found there that life was very cheap and that it was held in low esteem. You could buy a human being for $7.00 or one musket! That was cheaper than a cow. After having bought him you could work him, whip him, starve him, or eat him, according to your preference—and many did the latter. He returned a number of years later and found that the value of human life had risen tremendously. One could not buy a human being for $7.00 to beat or eat. In fact, you could not buy one for seven million dollars. Why? Because across the Fiji Islands there were 1,200 Christian chapels where the gospel of Christ had been proclaimed, and people had been taught that we are not our own; that we have been purchased with a price, not with silver and gold, but with the precious blood of Jesus Christ.

Remove Jesus Christ from the history of the world and the value of life would indeed be just as novelist Jack London's character Wolf Larsen put it: "Life? Bah! It has no value. Of the cheap things it is the cheapest."

Notes

1. Dionysius Exiguus, a Scythian monk, created the "Christian era" in A.D. 525. He began time with the birth of Christ at A.D. 1. He was later proven to be off by four years, which means that Christ was born four years before Christ! No matter, for the coming of the Son of God into our world demarcates the history of our world. It has never been the same since.

2. David Barrett and Todd Johnson, *Our Globe and How to Reach It: Seeing the World Evangelized by A.D. 2000 and Beyond* (Birmingham, AL: New Hope, 1990), 7.

3. Philip Schaff, *Person of Christ: The Miracle of History* (Boston: The American Tract Society, undated), 323, 328.

4. Friedrich Nietzsche, *The Birth of Tragedy and the Genealogy of Morals* (Garden City, NY: Doubleday Anchor Books, 1956), 170.

5. Quoted in Will Durant, *The Story of Philosophy* (New York: Simon & Schuster, 1953), 332.

6. Nietzsche, 185

7. Ibid., 168.

8. Friedrich Nietzsche, *The AntiChrist*, trans. by H.L. Mencken (Torrance, CA: The Noontide Press, 1980), 180.

9. Quoted in Durant, 322.

10. Ibid.

11. *Information Please Almanac, Atlas & Yearbook 1993* (Boston: Houghton Mifflin Co., 1993), 112.

12. Armin Robinson, ed., *The Ten Commandments: Ten Short Novels of Hitler's War Against the Moral Code*, with a preface by Herman Rauschning (New York: Simon & Schuster, 1943), ix.

13. Ibid., xi-xii.

14. Charles Lam Markmann, *The Noblest Cry* (New York: St. Martin's Press, 1965), 67.

15. David B. Barrett, *Cosmos, Chaos, and Gospel: A Chronology of World Evangelization from Creation to New Creation* (Birmingham, AL:

New Hope, 1987), 52 on Stalin (listed under year 1934), 60 on Mao (listed under year 1966).

16. Sherwood Eliot Wirt, *The Social Conscience of the Evangelical* (New York: Harper & Row, 1968), 37.

17. Henry Halley, *Halley's Bible Handbook* (Grand Rapids: Zondervan Publishing House, 1927, 1962), 141.

18. Ibid.

19. Robin Lane Fox, *Pagans and Christians* (San Francisco: Perennial Library, 1986, 1988), 47.

20. Ibid.

21. George Grant, *Third Time Around: A History of the Pro-Life Movement from the First Century to the Present* (Franklin, TN: Legacy, 1991, 1994), 20.

22. Fox, 343.

23. Help is only a phone call away. If you know someone who may need help like this, call 1–800-Bethany to reach someone who cares.

24. Wirt, 31.

25. Ibid., 30.

26. Grant, 38.

27. Ibid., 39.

28. Ibid., 46–47.

29. Fox, 48, emphasis mine.

30. Harald Stene Dehlin, *Pionerer i skort* [*Pioneers in Skirts*], passage trans. by Kirsti Saebo Newcombe (Oslo: Norsk Luthersk Forlag A/S, 1985), 67.

31. Adam Smith, *An Inquiry into the Nature and Causes of the Wealth of Nations* (Chicago: William Benton, 1956), 30.

32. Jo McGowan, "In India, They Abort Females," *Newsweek*, January 30, 1989, 12.

33. See Michael Breen, "Daughters Unwanted: Asian Quest for Boys Backed by Sex Tests, Abortions," *Washington Times*, February 13, 1993.

34. C.H. Spurgeon, *My Sermon Notes* (Grand Rapids: Christian Classics, 1884), 292.

35. Chuck Colson, *Breakpoint with Chuck Colson* (Washington, D.C.: Prison Fellowship, May 16, 1992).

36. Wirt, 10.

37. Isaac Asimov, *Asimov's Guide to the Bible,* Vol. 2, *The New Testament* (New York: Equinox Books, 1971), 489.

38. Fox, 296.

39. Ibid., 297–298, emphasis mine.

40. Ibid, 299.

41. Kenneth Scott Latourette, *A History of Christianity,* Vol. 1 (New York: Harper & Row, 1953, 1975), 246.

42. Wirt, 39.

43. *Liberty* (Sept./Oct. 1984).

44. See Will Durant, *Caesar and Christ,* 203, 207–208, 296, 306, 386, 422 for everyone listed excepted Pontius Pilate.

45. Barrett, *Cosmos, Chaos, and Gospel,* 21.

46. Durant, *Caesar and Christ,* 300.

"I Believe"

Michael Bauman

Michael Bauman is a professor of theology and culture and director of Christian Studies at Hillsdale College. He is also a lecturer and tutor in Renaissance literature and theology as well as associate dean at the Centre for Medieval and Renaissance Studies in Oxford. He has been book review editor for *The Journal of the Evangelical Theological Society* for eight years. He is the current president of the Evangelical Philosophical Society.

Formerly an editorial assistant at *Newsweek*, a pastor, chairman of the general education program at Northeastern Bible College, and an associate professor of religion at Fordham University, Dr. Bauman is the author of more than thirty articles and ten books, including *Pilgrim Theology: Taking the Path of Theological Discovery, Roundtable: Conversations with European Theologians, A Scripture Index to John Milton's* De Doctrina Christiana, *Milton's Arianism,* and editor or co-editor of *Are You Politically Correct? Debating America's Cultural Standards, The Best of the Manion Forum,* and Hillsdale's *Christian Vision* series.

"Faith might best be compared with love. Neither faith nor love is a point of view. If someone said: 'Tonight, I defend love as a point of view,' it would sound absurd. Love is a reality engendered by a relationship. Love develops from the encounter of two human beings. . . . It is felt to be a sweet domination of our being, and it stirs the desire to share our life with the loved one. It is the same as faith. The Other enters into our lives as the Lover. We then realize that we are not worthy of love, and we feel it to be an undeserved gift, a grace. The Other is God."

—J. T. Wiersma and J. W. Schulte Nordholt
The Apostles' Creed Interpreted in Words and Pictures

"What gives faith its seriousness and power is not that man makes a decision, nor even the way in which he makes it. . . . On the contrary, faith lives by its object. . . . The seri-

ousness and power of faith are the seriousness and power
of the truth, which is identical with God Himself."

—Karth Barth, *Credo*

I believe in God the Father almighty, maker of Heaven
and Earth;
And in Jesus Christ his only Son our Lord, who was conceived by the
Holy Spirit, born of the the virgin Mary,
suffered under Pontius Pilate,
was crucified, dead, and buried.
He descended into Hell.
The third day He rose again from the dead.
He ascended into Heaven, and sits at the right hand of
God the Father
almighty.
From there He shall come to judge the living and the
dead.
I believe in the the Holy Spirit;
the holy catholic church;
the communion of saints;
the forgiveness of sins;
the resurrection of the body;
and life everlasting.

—The Apostles' Creed

From its first word, the Apostles' Creed is personal. By
employing the word "I," it drives home with clarity the fact that
the faith of which it speaks is to be professed by each one of
us, singly and individually. Though others share it with us, the
faith we profess in the Apostles' Creed is expected to be our
own. When we recite the Apostles' Creed, we speak for ourselves and not for anyone else. When we say the Creed in
worship, we speak along with others, but not for them.

All who profess the Creed do so in light of the burden and
the privilege of being responsible selves, able to answer both
for what they are and for what they believe. The Apostles'
Creed presupposes that we are free to answer, able to answer,
and required to answer, the fundamental questions of life on
our own behalf, in our own voice. The Creed begins with a

person, a living soul, possessed of will and bound by duty, able to perceive truth and required to believe it. The more fully we contemplate the initial fact of the Creed, the more clearly we understand the nature and scope of our responsibility before God and our fellow creatures. We are called upon to declare, to profess, and to proclaim the content of our commitment. Like Luther before his interrogators, when we recite the Apostles' Creed we state clearly where we stand. We could not do otherwise and remain true to our calling.

Put differently, every Christian is expected to answer the question Jesus asked the man born blind, and to answer it in the same way: "Do you believe in the Son of Man?" Jesus asked. The reply He heard was the reply He required: "I believe" (John 9:35, 38). In the Apostles' Creed, we express our own faith because by it we either stand or fall. Our salvation rests upon our own belief, not that of others. In short, the Apostles' Creed presupposes that, as a child of God, you have the ability, the right, and the obligation to speak. And when you do, the first thing you ought to say is not simply "I," but "I believe."

Historically, the "I" to which the creed refers was, of course, the candidate for baptism, whose credible profession of faith was required before the rite of initiation could properly be administered. Part of that credible profession of faith included the candidate's own personal affirmation of belief in the Father, in the Son, and in the Holy Spirit. By such affirmations, the catechumens (persons receiving instruction in the fundamentals of Christianity) were, in Augustine's words, making with the mouth a profession of the personal faith they carried in their hearts (Augustine, *Treatise on Faith*, 321). The candidate for baptism made this three-fold profession of faith only after having pronounced a three-fold renunciation, which included a renunciation of the devil, of his service, and of his work. Thus, it becomes clear that the faith of the Apostles' Creed is the faith of a conversion, of an about-face, in which old habits and attachments have passed away and from which new loyalties and new commitments emerge.

By beginning as it does on a personal note, the Apostles' Creed differs from the original form of the Nicene Creed, which began with the words "We believe," words by which the

Nicene Creed represented itself not so much as the faith of a Christian but as the faith of the whole Church. This difference is instructive. "It gives expression to that strong consciousness of individual responsibility which has ever been the characteristic of Western Christianity, and brings home the facts of the faith to each simple believer who confesses them" (Maclear, *An Introduction to the Creeds,* 41).

But though much can and should be made of the "I" of faith, too much can (and often has been) made of it as well. This mistake, however, the Creed itself does not make. Though the Creed begins on the very personal note of individual belief, and though it presupposes a turning away of oneself from the old ways, the Creed does not leave the "I" of faith sequestered or alone. Before it closes, the Creed also affirms belief in the "holy catholic Church" and in "the communion of saints," of which the "I" is but a part, and not a part in isolation.

Thus, although the "I" of personal faith is properly fundamental, Christianity is not a privatistic religion. Ours is not a faith meant to be cloistered, least of all from other Christians. As Bishop Westcott once observed, while we each say, "I believe," we say it in conscious fellowship with those about us. This personal confession, he said, if we reflect upon it, makes our union with other Christians more real and more close because it articulates the deeply held commitments we freely share with one another.

Thus, while the faith of the Apostles' Creed is the faith of an individual, it is an individual faith shared by the Church everywhere and always. The creed inculcates what might be called an inclusive individualism, not isolationism. When we recite the Apostles' Creed, we speak for ourselves; but we speak in unison and in concert with the entire Church. The Apostles' Creed is simultaneously personal and ecumenical. If it were not, it would be a lesser creed.

The faith of the Apostles' Creed is not only personal in its subject, it is personal in its object as well. It is the belief of a person in a Person. We do not say, "I believe in something," but "I believe in God." The preposition "in" is of great importance because to believe in someone is to put your trust in him. In that light, the Christian faith is trusting in God as

Christ has revealed Him. Furthermore, when we profess our belief in God in the Apostles' Creed, we imply that the object of our faith is not merely something we know, but Someone that also knows us.

As commonly understood, the belief of which the Creed speaks is made up of both assent and trust. Assent is primarily cognitive and intellectual. It pertains to what we believe, to that which is the content of our faith. Trust indicates our attachment to the One in whom we believe, the object of our faith. The difference between these two dimensions of faith is sometimes depicted as the difference between saying "I believe that," (which is assent) and "I believe in," (which is trust). Put differently, faith is both a rational commitment and an act of confidence; it is both a knowing and a doing. To understand faith more completely, we must examine these two dimensions separately.

First, though theologians like Augustine, Anselm, and Aquinas have reached somewhat different conclusions on the matter, it seems to me that assent is normally prior to trust and is usually its foundation. That is, it seems on the whole more reasonable to expect one to believe that something is true and to have some rudimentary understanding of it before putting one's trust in it than it does to put one's trust in something before believing it is true and trying to understand it. But by no means is this sequence either normative or universal. Many Christians seem to have followed the opposite route. They seem rather to have believed in order to understand, not to understand in order to believe. To me, however, the better path lies in the other direction: Understand first. But to this issue the Creed does not expressly address itself. The Creed simply expresses faith, and it does so without stopping to specify either faith's normative sequence (if such there be) or its precise character.

Regarding its intellectual component, Christian faith is closely allied to reason and to truth. Conscious attachment to that which is opposed to knowledge, or to that which is somehow irrational, is not faith. It is credulity; it is a sin of the intellect. Credulity is not faith; credulity is superficial assent; it is indolence and mental malpractice. In short, credulity is an abdication of intellectual duty. It was not for the purpose of neglect that we were given minds. Those were invariably unproductive times for the Church when theology untied itself from the moorings of knowledge, of history, and of reason, as it seems to have done in our own age. But the faith professed in the Apostles' Creed is not so. Neither is that of the Bible. The Old Testament principle that "you should love the Lord your God with all your heart, with all your soul, and with all your strength" (Deut. 6:5), reappears in the New Testament with a very important addition: "and with all your *mind*" (Matt. 22:37, emphasis mine). That is why we are instructed to be ready to give a reason for the hope that is in us (1 Pet. 3:15).

Christian faith is neither ignorant nor unreasonable; rather, it is faith founded upon fact, specifically the hard facts of history. The foundations of the Christian faith are primarily historical, not speculative. Both Christian theology and the Bible from which it is drawn have history, not philosophy, as their foundation. We believe about the Christian faith what we do because at a particular time and place God intervened in human history. This intervention is unique, and in good theology it serves as the foundation for every important article of Christian assent. Virtually everything about God and about himself that any Christian can reasonably be asked to believe ought to be related carefully to these historical facts and be derived directly and reasonably from them. As Bishop Westcott observed, "We believe in God, and we declare His nature by recounting what He has done in the limits of time and space. We do not attempt to describe His essence or His attributes in abstract language. We speak of His works and through these we form in our human ways some conception of what He is" (Westcott, *The Historic Faith*, 25).

Thus, the Christian faith is not without its visible and historical indicators, and the Apostles' Creed itself directs our attention to them. The first of these indicators is creation, which the Creed mentions as the work of God. But most of the historical indicators to which the Creed refers pertain to the life and work of Jesus Christ, to events done at precisely articulated times and places (Christ "suffered under Pontius Pilate") and in carefully indicated sequences (Christ "was crucified,

died, and was buried; on the third day He rose again from the
dead"). Such affirmations indicate not only the "what" of belief, but also the "when" and the "why." One of the reasons we
trust Christ is because He rose from the dead—a fact that not
only helps to show why we believe, but which helps us to give
definition to our conception of the love of God and the power
of God.

By means of these historical indicators, the faith of the
Apostles' Creed looks back to the past, to the life of Jesus; and
it looks at the present, to the created world around us. It also
looks forward to the final forgiveness of sins, to the bodily
resurrection, and to eternal life. It does so because it has seen
in Christ, in space and time, historical indications of things to
come. Thus, contrary to popular misconceptions, faith is based
on historical knowledge; not ignorance, not groundless hope,
not empty wishes. Paul's way of saying this was to assert that
he knew the One in whom he had trusted and, because he
did, he was convinced that his future was secure (2 Tim. 1:12).
John strikes a similar note by confirming to his readers that
what he writes to them are things that he himself had seen with
his own eyes, heard with his own ears, and touched with his
own hands (1 John 1:1–3). Or, to echo James, if faith without
works is dead, faith without knowledge is superstition. Christian
faith is not at all the same as, nor is it nurtured by, either the
absence of knowledge or a flight from reason. Orthodoxy en-
tails historical facts and sound thinking. It involves knowledge,
and knowledge—real knowledge—involves truth. This truth is
the food both of our minds and our souls. The faith of the
creed, because it is a sound faith, presupposes truth and a
rational order, things which, if they are to be properly understood, require a disciplined mind. The one who has no conception of, or commitment to, a rational order is not a person of
faith; he is the target of every charlatan who comes down the
pike. Many Christians, nevertheless, though quite properly in-
clined to use their minds constructively and effectively in all
other affairs, decline to do so in matters of religion. Their
reluctance engenders the daunting plethora of difficulties associated with ignorance, such as spiritual poverty and doubt.
But faith seeks understanding. Theological ignorance, indeed

ignorance of any kind, is not a mark of faith, but of indolence and credulity. It is not the door to blessing but to theological barbarism.

Second, as we indicated above, faith is not a mental virtue only. What counts is not simply one's possession and understanding of faith, but also its use. In fact, if you do not use your faith, if you do not commit yourself to it and act upon it, you probably do not have it. To have a faith and not to use it, to have a faith and not be committed to the object of that faith, is not the faith of the Creed; it is delusion. Christian faith is not only knowing, it is doing. Christian faith requires more than clear thinking and a positive intellectual content; it requires that you vigorously lay hold of that in which you believe, that you give yourself to it. Thus, while sound thinking and a commitment to fact constitute the intellectual side of faith and serve to protect the believer from making unworthy and misguided attachments, the trust or commitment side of faith is that which gives it life and prevents it from being a merely mental exercise.

Faith is energetic and active. Because faith is a living, courageous confidence in the grace of God, it does not fearfully or fretfully grope about in the dark, unable or unwilling to think or do anything on its own. Instead, when it is healthy and well formed, faith is eager, energetic and daring; it is willing to suffer hardship for the sake of the truth to which it has committed itself. In short, to have a faith and to live it is an inestimable and energizing privilege.

But Christian faith is not doubt-free; no position in life is. Atheists and agnostics have their bouts with doubt, just like their Christian counterparts. As Joseph Ratzinger explains,

> However vigorously [the unbeliever] may assert that he is a pure positivist, who has long left behind him supernatural temptations and weaknesses, and now accepts only what is immediately certain, he will never be free of the secret uncertainty whether positivism really has the last word. Just as the believer is choked by the salt water of doubt constantly washed into his mouth by the ocean of uncertainty, so the non-believer is troubled by doubts about his unbelief, and the real totality of the world which he has made up his mind to explain as a self-

contained whole.... Just as the believer knows himself to be constantly threatened by unbelief, which he must experience as a continual temptation, so for the unbeliever faith remains a temptation and a threat to his apparently permanently closed world. In short, there is no escape from the dilemma of being a man. Anyone who makes up his mind to evade the uncertainty of belief will have to experience the uncertainty of belief, which can never finally eliminate for certain the possibility that belief may after all be the truth. It is not until belief is rejected that its unrejectability becomes evident.... [B]oth the believer and the unbeliever share, each in his own way, doubt and belief, if they do not hide away from themselves and from the truth of their being (*Introduction to Christianity*, 20, 21).

All persons have doubts, and the doubts that arise in the mind of a Christian are not unlike those that arise in the minds of all persons who think seriously about life. But the wisest among us realize that the mere presence of doubt is not, nor ever can be, determinative. They have learned to doubt their doubts, not simply their beliefs. They also have learned that doubt, when squarely faced, is an avenue to stronger and more mature faith, even though for the moment it is painful or grievous. Doubts, when confronted and conquered, are the proof of faith. In that light, the faith of the Apostles' Creed has been proven. Throughout its many centuries of use, the Creed has been the occasion for doubts of various sorts, not one of which is without answer or remedy. Like those who profess it, the Creed has emerged strong and unbroken from the smoke and battle of confrontation with doubt and unbelief. In so doing, the Creed and its adherents have proven the truth of Paul's observation that we are more than conquerors in Christ (Rom. 8:37), an observation which implies that not only are we victorious in the battles of faith, but we emerge from those battles stronger than we were when we entered.

Nor do people often understand that doubt itself has within it a distinctive element of faith. When one begins to doubt one's beliefs and begins sincerely to question the answers at hand, one does so only on the belief that better answers are both possible and worth having. If you believe no answers are possible, you cease to search for them. Thus, to travel hopefully is an act of intellectual faith. To pursue the answers to questions raised by doubt is compatible only with faith, but not with faith's opposites—the intellectual despair that denies that answers can be had, on the one hand, and the spiritual complacency and self-satisfaction that delude one into thinking that one's beliefs require no further scrutiny or refinement, on the other. Christian faith is neither self-generated nor self-sustained. It carries neither its origin nor its norm within itself. For those things the believer must look to God as He has been revealed in history—in Christ and in words in Scripture. Christian faith arises in response: in response to God's revelation, in response to God's initiative, and in response to God's offer.

In other words, the source of Christian faith is also its goal. The faith that ends in commitment to God begins with the will and grace of God. Faith is the echo which God's call creates in the hearts of those who believe. Thus, faith is first of all a work of God and only secondarily a human response. Concerning faith's benefits, Thomas Aquinas long ago correctly perceived that Christian faith not only is a requirement of the first order but that it yields four great advantages. By means of faith, (1) "the soul is wedded to God;" (2) "eternal life is begun in us;" (3) we "know whatever is necessary for living well;" and (4) "we conquer temptations (Sermon Conferences, 19, 21).

To summarize, the faith of which the creed speaks is a personal faith, personal both in its subject and its Object. This faith is also the faith of conversion, indicating both a rejection of the old ways and a hearty attachment to the new. As such, the faith of the Apostles' Creed is comprised of two elements— assent and trust. But these two elements, though lively and strong, do not render faith entirely doubt-free. In that respect, Christian belief is like all other serious human commitments. Of the two basic components of faith, the former (assent) indicates the content of belief; the latter (trust) indicates our relationship to its object. That is, we believe the doctrine; we believe in God. Thus, while the subject of faith is the individual Christian, its proper Object is not simply the Creed, but God as He is revealed in Christ. The God revealed in Christ is the Object of faith, and in relation to Him we exercise our trust.